Eisenhower and Social Security

Eisenhower and Social Security

The Origins of the Disability Program

Dominick Pratico

February 7, 2001

Writers Club Press

San Jose New York Lincoln Shanghai

Eisenhower and Social Security
The Origins of the Disability Program

Writers Club Press
an imprint of iUniverse.com, Inc.

For information address:
iUniverse.com, Inc.
5220 S 16th, Ste. 200
Lincoln, NE 68512
www.iuniverse.com

ISBN: 0-595-17983-5

Printed in the United States of America

For Beaky and the Pork Chop;
And the Tough Guy, who came later, of course

Contents

Forward

One measure of a civilized society is the way that it cares for its sick or injured. Few of us can conceive of a point in time when we might not be able to care for our own needs or those of our families. But we are all just a car accident or misstep on an icy sidewalk away from dire consequences. Crippling illness is indiscriminate; strokes and cancer affect the rich and the poor alike. These unpleasant possibilities are seldom considered. "That will never happen to me," is a common mantra. Anything more is considered paranoia or extreme pessimism.

In the 19th century, Americans did not believe in the federal government as a charitable institution. The prevailing ideology was that local government agencies or private charitable organizations were best suited to address social welfare issues in their immediate communities. Programs could be customized to address specific local needs. But the existing programs in the early 20th century were woefully inadequate to meet the demands placed upon them. In most instances, the extended family was still responsible for supporting the elderly or the disabled. The American self-image was still that of the hardy frontiersman or the shrewd businessman. The individual and the family were expected to provide for disability, retirement or death. Herbert Hoover maintained his faith in this outmoded ideology, even though the Great Depression made it abundantly clear that the times had passed it by. Franklin Roosevelt and the New Dealers took great strides in addressing the thorny issues of social insurance. The Social Security Act, as originally passed in 1935, was a progressive piece of legislation, but it had many shortcomings, the most glaring of which was the absence of disability insurance.

Dwight D Eisenhower, at first, would appear an unlikely proponent of social disability insurance. Eisenhower is remembered for many accomplishments, such as his military leadership in World War II and his two terms as President of the United States. The amendments to the Social Security Act that he signed into law are seen as a mere footnote in his presidency, even though these reforms of the Social Security law had sweeping national implications and have affected the lives of every American since the 1950's. Eisenhower's major accomplishments as president in foreign and domestic policy seemed remote to the average person, as there were no immediately perceptible changes or benefits to the individual. Advantages earned for the nation as a whole, such as national security, can seem hollow in the abstract. As an ignored dependent underclass, the sick and the disabled had far more pressing concerns than blocking the advances of communism in Europe. What made Franklin Roosevelt a champion of the common man was that his New Deal reforms were concrete and their impact was felt directly by the masses. The Social Security disability program enacted during the Eisenhower Administration affected millions in the same way. But Eisenhower's legacy is not that of a social reformer who rescued the sick and injured. The reasons for this, as well as the origins of Social Security disability program itself, are equally compelling and will be the focus of this tome.

CHAPTER ONE

The Social Security Act of 1935

The overall economic collapse brought on by the Great Depression (1929-1941) forced Americans to confront the absence of a safety net for the common wage earner in the existing economic system. Only the wealthiest Americans had the ability to insulate themselves against a sudden loss of income due to old age or disability. When facing such a crisis, the poorest Americans were dependent upon family members, the inadequate poor relief system, or simple charity.

By the 1920's, legislators were aware that the aged segment of society was increasing and having difficulty finding jobs. Urbanization, the decrease in self-employment, the loosening of family ties due to greater mobility, the resistance to charity, and the universal disdain for the poor house forced legislators to start considering remedies to these problems. Nothing happened, however, until The Great Depression provided the impetus for government involvement in social reforms. Aged men of moderate wealth suddenly found themselves penniless in the wake of the stock market crash in 1929. The problems of the aged poor were no longer restricted to the lower classes.[1]

The need for old age insurance was part of the general movement for social insurance, labeled "social security," in the 1930's. Franklin Roosevelt's mind-set was different from that of most politicians of the day. He was a progressive Hudson Valley patrician who had inherited his wealth, not a ruthless businessman who had earned his every penny. He saw himself as fortunate by accident of birth; his own experience with polio, contracted at age thirty-nine, showed him just how precarious life and health could be. As a result, Roosevelt was more inclined to be philanthropic, but he did not favor outright federal charity. He envisioned a progressive program of social legislation. His record as Governor of New York spoke for itself: a system of comprehensive unemployment relief, a program of industrial welfare, conservation of public energy sources and attention to the "forgotten man at the bottom of the economic pyramid."[2]

The idea of contributory pension systems was not new in the 1930's. Old age pensions had existed in Europe since the 1880's, when Otto Von Bismarck put such a system into place in Germany. Theodore Roosevelt's Progressive Party platform in 1912 called for old age pensions, but the problem was that any viable plan would require federal oversight because state legislation concerning old age pensions was sporadic and ineffective to meet the needs of such a large segment of the population. The migratory tendencies of ordinary workers complicated any state-run system. This was also an obstacle to unemployment insurance. Federalism severely limited the effectiveness of social welfare programs as local, state and federal components continually clashed at cross sections of purpose. Federal support was not forthcoming in 1912 and nothing came of the idea. Until 1932, no serious consideration was given to enacting a federal program of social insurance. The matter was repeatedly relegated to the states to resolve. The Democratic Party platform in 1932, designed to garner maximum support for Franklin Roosevelt, promised relief, including social insurance, to the greatest number of individuals afflicted by the Great Depression.[3]

Staring into the maw of the Great Depression, Roosevelt did not want to create a social program that appeared ad hoc or superficial, like much of the rest of his New Deal programs. He wanted a system that truly worked and would be able to withstand attacks that it was socialist in nature. He also needed to counter the growing popularity of Dr. Francis Townsend and his scheme for old age pensions.

Townsend was an unsuccessful physician who at the age of 67 had nothing to show for his life's work. His savings were insufficient to finance his retirement. In response to his own situation, as well as to those who were even less fortunate than himself, he became a vocal proponent for the federal government to pay every person over the age of sixty $200 per month. The only conditions were that beneficiaries retire from gainful work and spend the entire $200 each month. The pension would be financed by a two-percent tax on business transactions, which would be paid into a trust fund. While the Townsend Plan made good press in the midst of the Great Depression, the fact of the matter was that it was more of a recovery program than a pension plan. It called for taking money away from the young and giving it the old in a fiscally irresponsible manner. The United States had a national income of $40 billion annually and Townsend wanted to give away $24 billion of it as compensation to only 9 percent of the population. Weak economics aside, it was a very attractive notion to an impoverished and starving nation.[4]

In Roosevelt's opinion, the easiest way to derail Townsend, and at the same time create a sound pension program, would be to establish such a system financed through workers' and employers' contributions rather than from general tax revenues. On June 8, 1934, Roosevelt issued an Executive Order creating the Cabinet Committee on Economic Security (CCES) to study alternatives on the issue of social insurance. The CCES was comprised of Secretary of the Treasury Henry Morganthau, Jr., Secretary of Agriculture Henry Wallace, Attorney General Homer Cummings and Federal Emergency Relief Administrator Harry Hopkins. Roosevelt also appointed Rexford Tugwell, Professor Edwin Witte, Arthur Altmeyer, Paul Rauschenbush and Elizabeth Brandeis to the CCES. Secretary of Labor Frances Perkins served as Chairwoman. Perkins made it clear from the onset that her objective was not to find a way to ensure complete economic security, but only to provide partial compensation for economically catastrophic events. Roosevelt and his advisors saw a viable social insurance program as a means of preventing the perennial recurrence of economic collapse.[5]

On January 15, 1935, the CCES reported to the President and provided the basic outline of the Social Security Act. The CCES concluded that Americans perceived security as an assured income, so the CCES sought to insure that every employable person had the opportunity to work for a decent wage. The type of employment, public or private, was not controlling. If public employment was necessary, than a transition program could be initiated to move the worker eventually into the private sector. This would soon become the Works Project Administration (WPA). But the impersonal market forces made no provision for illness, disability, old age or the needs of survivors. Economic opportunity was the true means to prosperity, either through wages or a program of social insurance funded through the contributions of the workers themselves. The program needed only to redistribute income, not equalize it.[6]

Both Roosevelt and the CCES agreed that federal oversight of the program was necessary. Roosevelt demanded universal coverage for all through old age, survivor and disability benefits, from the cradle to the grave, and that participation in the program be mandatory. He also insisted upon both employer and employee contributions to ensure that no public monies would be required as a supplement. Secretary Perkins and the CCES disagreed, believing that the logistical and administrative problems of what the President wanted were insurmountable. In addition, they argued that implementing a payroll tax would mean that those who could least afford it would finance the program. Roosevelt accepted this assessment, but he still insisted that the program be implemented his way. The income tax rate was very low in 1935; 95 percent of Americans paid no income tax at all. Even though a payroll tax would penalize the poor by diminishing their take-home pay, it was essential, Roosevelt believed, because the alternative, to fund the program through general revenues, was a fiscally questionable approach that would leave the program vulnerable to partisan politics. National reinsurance plans were also considered, but were discarded for the same reason. Under such programs, private insurance companies would be required to pool their resources and offer old age, survivor and disability pensions instead of the federal government. The insurance companies, under guidelines established by the federal government, would run the programs with the expectation of earning profits and federal monies from the general revenues would be used to pay the administrative costs. Reinsurance plans left workers vulnerable not only to partisan politics, but to the coldly impersonal treatment of an insurance company only concerned with the bottom line. Roosevelt was convinced that the payroll tax remained the only viable alternative to circumvent the greedy, pork barrel tendencies of Congress and the private insurance concerns that would seek to exploit worker misfortunes. Roosevelt believed that workers needed to be guaranteed the legal, moral and political right to collect their old age pensions. By limiting congressional authority over the program's funding, the program itself would be insulated against any future attempts to dismantle it.[7]

Roosevelt's economic recovery programs rested on the assumption that a just society could be secured by imposing a welfare state on a capitalist foundation. Without significantly altering the system of private profit, the authority of the federal government could be exerted not only to regulate business, but also to provide pensions for the elderly and give relief to the needy. Roosevelt's plan was to marry the American profit system to assistance for the aged and, in the process, render working class life less precarious. But this method would still not guarantee everyone a pension. An individual would have to pay into the system to receive benefits, which meant a person first needed a job. The Social Security bill failed to address the concerns of the neediest segments of society. This was intentional, but with an eye towards a greater goal. During its deliberations, the CCES concluded that many were simply too old or too poor for the federal government to help. Responsibility for the severely disenfranchised was to remain with state or local programs, an apparatus allegedly better equipped to deal with such individuals. Social Security was conceived as a means to eradicate one of the sources of poverty rather than to treat its symptoms. The program would be more concerned with preventing the next depression than ending the current one. A long-term base of security for the nation's industrial population was the intended goal, not an immediate cure-all for the plight of the disenfranchised. This principle, in conjunction with the political climate, led Roosevelt and the CCES to omit any reference to a disability benefits from their proposal to Congress. American social insurance was conceived as a whole, but Roosevelt conceded that it would have to be enacted incrementally. Roosevelt hoped that the Social Security system would evolve over time to meet the demands of society, and that someday in the future the program could be expanded to include disabled individuals. He believed that the perseverance of liberal government for at least another ten years was necessary for this to happen.[8]

On January 17, 1935, the Social Security bill was introduced into both houses of Congress. The proposed legislation was an easy target for detractors. The "Lunatic Fringe," as Roosevelt referred to Dr. Francis Townsend, Father Charles Coughlin, Huey Long, and their followers, had a field day because the plan for implementation was not clearly defined. The bill submitted to Congress included only old age and survivor benefits, coupled with a program of unemployment insurance and block grants to state welfare programs. The Social Security bill involved workers, their employers, and the federal government in a joint effort to provide some guaranteed income in people's later years. The Roosevelt administration touted the bill as a means for maintaining acceptable standards of living and spending power for aged citizens at no added cost to the government. The program's compulsory nature made it an attractive alternative to the public dole.[9]

The Social Security bill passed the House of Representatives on April 19, 1935, by a vote of 371 to 33. Many Congressmen who voted in favor of the bill did so in spite of their own reservations concerning the long-term viability of the program and the potential fallout at the polls over levying a new tax in time of economic hardship. However, conservative Republicans and anti-New Deal Democrats stalled the bill in the Senate. Frustrated, Roosevelt refused to let Congress adjourn for the sweltering summer without passing his social legislative agenda. The Social Security bill finally passed the Senate on June 19, 1935, by a vote of 76 to 6, but difficulties still remained. As indicated by the vote, opponents of the bill did not want to go on record as opposing the measure, so they contrived to hold it up in conference committee over the Senate's adoption of an amendment to exempt employers with industrial pension plans from the program. Roosevelt opposed the exclusion of any group of workers from the program as impractical and a dangerous precedent. The program depended upon a large number of contributors to generate sufficient revenue and keep the tax rate low by spreading out the overhead cost, all of which would be endangered if different segments of the working population could opt out of the program. In the end, the Senate yielded to the President, and the Social Security Act was signed into law on August 15, 1935.[10]

The Social Security bill passed the Democratic controlled Congress mostly because it was Roosevelt's wish and because of unexpected support from Republicans who refused to follow the party line. Congressman Joseph Martin, representing an impoverished section of Massachusetts, and other Republicans voted in favor of the bill because they believed that it was the responsibility of the federal government to see to the welfare of workers whom, as young men, had helped build the United States. They believed that it was wrong to let young men pass into old age and then abandon them. They believed that Social Security would evolve to become just compensation for these men's efforts. Many Republican legislators believed otherwise, yet had no desire to debate the finer points of the bill and resorted instead to well-poisoning tactics, such as predicting that Social Security would lead to the decline of American civilization by making the currently disastrous economic situation worse. But even the harshest critics of the program, such as Congressmen John Taber (R-NY), Daniel Reed (R-NY), James Wadsworth (R-NY) and Senator Daniel

Hastings (R-DE), made sure to be recorded as proponents of Social Security. They feared taking a beating at the polls if they opposed aid to the aged indigent. These legislators had little faith that Social Security would alleviate the financial strain on the elderly and actually believed that it would make the current economic situation worse, yet they voted for it to preserve their political careers.[11]

The Social Security Act, Public Law 74-271, as adopted in 1935, was, by modern standards, an extremely conservative piece of legislation. However, it was the only viable alternative given the political and judicial climate in 1935. Many were excluded from the Social Security program before they even had a chance to participate. Tax collections began in 1937 and the first monthly payments were not scheduled to occur until 1942. People who retired before 1937 were out of luck, and those who retired before monthly payments commenced received a minimal, one time, lump sum payment that averaged $58.06. Others worked at occupations that were not covered by the program, such as self-employed professionals, farmers and domestic servants. The problem of farmers was unique. Farmers often kept poor payroll records for their employees, if they paid them at all. Many were live-in hired hands who received as compensation only room and board. Many farmers could not afford the burden of paying the Social Security tax and were suspicious of federal authority in general. As part of a compromise with those legislators representing rural areas, farmers were excluded from the program, along with those who worked for them. A similar approach was applied concerning domestic servants. Women were still expected to manage the household, but it was assumed that housewives lacked the ability to properly file the paperwork needed for Social Security tax withholding from the payroll of the household staff.[12]

Any thought of including health insurance coverage or disability insurance was killed by the American Medical Association and private insurance interests. The medical profession claimed that the business and scientific incentives inherent in the current method of medical practice would be stunted by federal oversight. A great deal of time, effort and money was spent in establishing a medical career, and, according to the doctors, the potential profit was justifiable recompense and helped finance research. In essence, doctors did not want to become federal employees. Doctors feared that national health or disability insurance would be the first step toward socialized medicine.[13]

At its inception, old age insurance suffered bitter attacks from the business community. Alfred Sloan of General Motors, James Donnelly of the Illinois Manufacturers' Association, Charles Denby of the American Bar Association and George Chandler of the Ohio Chamber of Commerce, among others, denounced the Social Security program. They condemned the additional tax to be levied on employers as an anchor around the neck of economic progress. They argued that the lack of recurring payments or substantial one-time payments offered no true financial security and thus no lasting contribution to the economy. Moreover, they pointed out that no allowance was made for the independent elderly or the indigent and the glaring lack of any disability or health insurance coverage. The regressive tax was branded as cruel; the poor paid the cost of keeping the poor. Despite this relentless criticism, Roosevelt defended the program. He had cashed in a great deal of political capital in order to establish a social insurance program in America. He expected the program to pay modest dividends in the present, but, for the long term, he envisioned a reduction in federal expenditures. A viable social insurance program would result in smaller cash grants to the states for the maintenance of welfare programs. Roosevelt also pointed out that the federal government had finally recognized the social rights of individuals. The overriding complaint at the time was that the Social Security Act made more political sense than economic.[14]

Not that Social Security was immune from attacks on political grounds. The rest of the world, particularly Europe, was moving quickly toward faceless regimentation, but individual enterprise was still cherished in America. Many New Deal reforms were perceived as an attempt to undermine and destroy American individualism. The Republican Party in the 1930's was in a state of disorganization, reeling from the growing strength of Roosevelt and the New Deal Democrats. Some Democrats broke with Roosevelt and cooperated with Republicans to forge a bipartisan opposing bloc. Conservative Democrats, such as Vice President John Nance Garner of Texas, former New York Governor Alfred Smith and Senator Harry Byrd of Virginia, aligned themselves with like-minded Republicans such as Senator A. Harry Moore of New Jersey. Together, they tried to use this "threat" to the American way of life as a rallying point. Over the spring and summer of 1935, Republican legislators had argued weakly against the Social Security bill in the House and Senate and then wilted under Roosevelt's influence. They turned to scare tactics in the 1936 presidential election. Republican orators engaged in a concentrated, organized effort to smear Roosevelt in the 1936 campaign by denigrating the Social Security Act in every possible way. The innocent was made sinister. Republican candidate Alf Landon, the Governor of Kansas, charged that Roosevelt was "strangling free enterprise" and that he ultimately planned to rob Americans of their basic freedoms of religion, speech and property ownership. Hearst newspapers warned that the President regularly took the counsel of communists, and the *Chicago Tribune* reported that Moscow had ordered its American agents to back the New Deal. The assignment of social security numbers and ID cards to every worker was condemned as the first step on the road toward fascism. A parallel was drawn to Europeans who had to carry police cards. Roosevelt's critics charged that reducing each person to a nine-digit number dehumanized the individual, and that the Social Security program invited the federal government to interfere in the daily lives of ordinary citizens and literally to steal money from the average worker's pockets through payroll taxes. Passage of the Social Security Act had punctuated the decline in the influence of industrial leaders over the federal government. They hoped to recoup some of their political losses by tearing down Roosevelt. The President retaliated in a stinging speech delivered at Madison Square Garden in New York City on election eve. He scolded the proponents of avarice in a time of want and skewered his critics by pointing out that many of the Republicans deriding him in the press had actually voted for the Social Security Act in 1935. The Republican decision to use Social Security as a weapon turned out to be a major tactical blunder as their voting records from the summer of 1935 came back to haunt them. Dissident elements in the Democratic Party were sternly rebuked by Roosevelt's victory in 1936. The public, as a whole, was enthusiastic about Social Security and the backlash against Republican moneyed interests only brought more support to Roosevelt and his ideals.[15]

As the economy slowly improved in the late 1930's, the public also returned to previously held values emphasizing individualism and personal success. By 1937, conservatives were arguing that the time for reform had passed. The established conviction that business was the best engine to drive the economy reasserted itself. Genuine compassion for the victims of the Great Depression yielded to feelings of contempt. The burden of the dependent underclass became too great an economic and moral weight to carry. Those with jobs or other independent means of income likened the Depression to a sort of Judgement Day that fiscally divided the saved and the unsaved. In 1937, WPA Director Harry Hopkins wrote that America had become "bored with the poor, the unemployed and the insecure."[16] The voices that believed in economic prosperity as the true solution to poverty became louder. Healthy businesses providing subsistence level jobs were seen as the proper relief for the poor, aged and disabled. While the mood of the nation was against further reforms by 1937, people did not want any of the previous reforms repealed. Little new legislation could be enacted due to the sharp division between conservative and New Deal Democrats. At the same time, existing reforms could not be undone. This was emphasized on May 24, 1937, when the Supreme Court ruled 7-2 in the case of *Helvering v. Davis* that the Social Security Act was constitutional.[17]

Despite validation by the Supreme Court, the long-term viability of the Social Security Act was still in doubt in 1938. At its inception, Social Security was a complicated piece of social machinery that few people outside of the President and its planners understood. The expansion of federal authority at the expense of big business and the minimal payments to beneficiaries in return left the program vulnerable. The prognosis was that Social Security would not survive the seven years it would take to phase in the system completely. The program needed a shot in the arm and men like Arthur Altmeyer, the Chairman of the Social Security Board, recommended an expansion of entitlement categories. The greater the number of individuals who stood to benefit from the program, the greater public and legislative support it would receive. Simply put, there was strength in numbers. Roosevelt agreed with this assessment; the only question was how to proceed.[18]

The Republicans experienced a resurgence after the 1938 elections as the public, frightened by Roosevelt's attempt to "pack" the Supreme Court, wanted to restore some of the traditional checks and balances. The Democrats lost 81 seats in the House and 8 seats in the Senate. While the Democrats still held majorities in both houses of Congress, the election results placed an increased emphasis on the President's need for old-line Democratic support. Conservative and New Deal Democrats realized that they needed to mend fences if they were to succeed at the polls in 1940. The President used this set of circumstances to his advantage.[19]

In 1939, Roosevelt sold his expansion of the Social Security program to legislators through a combination of pragmatism and coercion. If fellow Democrats wanted his support at the next election, they would have to vote to liberalize the program's entitlements. The payoff to legislators was that they could campaign and take credit for easing the financial burdens of the aged and their dependents. Legislators chafed at being outmaneuvered because few of them wanted to go on record as being unsympathetic to the plight of the aged. The center held because of a grudging respect for the President, not faith in the program. The August 1939 amendments to the Social Security Act, which protected the insured worker's family, were crucial to the program's survival. Dependent spouses and widows, children under the age of

18, and surviving aged parents became entitled to Social Security benefit payments, and trust fund surpluses allowed for a reduction in the Social Security tax rate. More benefits at a cheaper cost made the Democrats look good while endearing Social Security to the masses. In addition, on January 1, 1940, monthly benefit payments were initiated, two years ahead of schedule. This not only robbed critics of one of their major criticisms of the program, but it also enhanced the financial stability of the aged and their dependents.[20]

Social Security was created to be self-sustaining, and under the watchful eyes of Treasury Secretary Henry Morganthau, Jr., the Social Security trust fund deliberately amassed a surplus of contributions. Morganthau invested the surplus in government bonds and the interest alone generated one-third of the revenue needed to keep the program operating. The employer and employees paid the remaining two-thirds of the costs. Government subsidies would never be needed. Concerns over the economic impact of such a large degree of spending power being removed from the national economy were answered simply with increases in benefit payments and categories of entitlement. This provided a means to return the monies to circulation. Benefit payments were never intended to be a person's sole income in retirement, but a supplement to a nest egg or other source of income.[21]

Roosevelt entered the presidential campaign of 1940 fully backing all of his New Deal reforms. Roosevelt's adversary in this campaign was Wendell Willkie, a moderate whose experience was in business, not government. The Republican platform in 1940 embraced Social Security in an attempt to tap into the popularity of the 1939 amendments to the Act. In fact, Willkie called for further extending Social Security in order "to provide jobs for every man and woman in the United States willing to work and to continue public relief to those who could not work." Willkie hastened the integration of Social Security into the mainstream by helping to instill a sense of social responsibility in the business community. Frances Perkins appraised this turn of events as highly favorable to the future viability of Social

Security: "Well, God's holy name be praised," she commented. "No matter who gets elected we've won."[22]

The Social Security Act and the 1939 amendments were intended to achieve a more just society by recognizing that the needs of many Americans had gone unheeded. Yet this was still only a partial revolution. The ranks of the middle class would swell in the 1940's while many other disenfranchised Americans, such as sharecroppers, slum dwellers and most Blacks, were systematically barred from the benefits of reform. Social Security addressed many difficult problems, but for each one it solved, it created equally vexing new ones. Outside of Roosevelt and Perkins, there had been no outcry for a social insurance program from influential policymakers. However, reformers took advantage of the Great Depression to enact a progressive agenda of longstanding duration.[23]

From 1936 to 1945, Congress reluctantly went along with old age insurance. The program was ignored or criticized incessantly. Senator Sheridan Downey (D-CA) built a political career based upon attacking Social Security. Herbert Hoover charged Roosevelt and the New Dealers with currency manipulation and fascist dictation to business, labor and agriculture. But by 1945, memories of the Great Depression were fading. As the Truman administration set to the task of demobilizing the armed forces and restoring a peacetime economy, social insurance issues were largely ignored. This unintended legislative inertia aided in ensuring Social Security's long term viability. As national economic conditions gradually improved, so did individual prosperity. More and more workers who had watched their own parents literally work themselves into their graves now retired comfortably on Social Security. Younger workers were relieved of the financial burden of caring for aged parents and were shown that one day, they too would have assured income for their own retirement. Accordingly, most working people strongly supported Social Security. By 1950, more than 12 million Americans were over 65, compared to 3 million in 1900 (a growth rate 3 times that of the rest of the population). Legislators began to reflect the sentiments of these constituents and by the end of the

Truman administration in 1953, Social Security became the nation's most popular social insurance program. In the shadows of this national love affair with Social Security, however, labor leaders were still unable to make any gains on the behalf of disabled workers.[24]

In 1943, Social Security administrators had tried, unsuccessfully, to enact a program of *temporary* disability insurance as part of an extension of Social Security. State and local disability programs undermined the need for a federal program and business leaders refused to accept even a minute increase in the Social Security tax rate. It was cheaper for employers to offer temporary disability coverage themselves as part of their employee benefit package. The Social Security Advisory Council (SSAC) started pushing for a program of permanent, or long-term, disability benefits, in 1948. Congressman Wilbur Mills (D-AR), an influential member and later chairman of the House Ways and Means Committee, impeded the efforts of the SSAC. He made a career of blocking disability and health care legislation, believing that they were state, local or private matters and not the business of the federal government.[25]

The idea of *temporary* disability benefits was soon abandoned in favor of *permanent* disability benefits, but proposals for such benefits became caught in the crossfire of the national health care debate. In 1951, Wilbur Cohen, one of the assistants to the head of the Social Security Board, believed it was possible to take advantage of the social insurance consensus that was in favor of old age insurance and use it to implement a plan for national health insurance. His idea was to provide health insurance only to Social Security beneficiaries and to have the Social Security Administration oversee the program. It could easily be sold to Congress as an extension of Social Security, a program ascending in popularity, rather than as an overhaul of the existing health care system. Oscar Ewing, the head of the Federal Security Agency, liked the idea and proposed Cohen's plan to Congress.[26]

But before Congress would act on Ewing's health insurance initiative, legislators wanted to resolve the ongoing debate over disability insurance. Temporary disability was politically unpalatable; opponents complained that it encouraged workers with minor injuries to refrain from seeking gainful employment. However, an entitlement program based on permanent disability due to severe illness or injury was seen as viable. The House Ways and Means Committee endorsed the measure in spite of Wilbur Mills and the bill passed the House itself in 1951, only to be killed in the Senate Finance Committee. The bill faced a powerful adversary in the American Medical Association (AMA).[27]

The AMA linked the issue of disability to national health insurance. A permanent disability benefit program was perceived as the entering wedge for a program of national health insurance, which the doctors saw as the first step down the slippery slope into socialized medicine. According to the AMA, it was inevitable that the federal government would hire doctors to make disability determinations, then coerce them into going along with national health insurance, and before anyone realized it, doctors would be regimented federal employees. The AMA argued that welfare was superior to a federal disability program because individual localities were better suited to see to the needs of each community. Legislators, wary of offending the doctors and their money, shied away from federal disability insurance programs.[28]

By the end of the Truman Administration in January 1953, the Social Security tax rate was below 6 percent. Social Security benefits compared favorably to private insurance because Social Security covered more workers than all other pension plans in the United States, even though benefit payments were made at a lower rate. The saving grace was that it cost less than private insurance to administer. All of this was accomplished without sacrificing the American virtue of individuals working toward a common good and Social Security remained in sync with the American capitalist system of private profit. In contrast to the situation in 1945, the politicians were falling all over themselves by 1953 to claim credit for Social Security's passage and to praise it with no end. While the prevailing sentiment, partly orchestrated by the AMA, was against amending the Social Security Act, forward-thinking politicians understood that the Social Security program required expansion. There were still millions of Americans who existed outside the safety net, both aged and disabled. The only question was how to proceed.[29]

References: Chapter One

1) Paul Douglas, *In the Fullness of Time: The Memoirs of Paul H Douglas* (New York: Harcourt Brace Jovanich, 1972), 69; William Leuchtenburg, *Franklin D Roosevelt and the New Deal, 1932-1940* (New York: Harper and Row, 1963), xii and 1-3.

2) Douglas, 71-75; Leuchtenburg, 4-5.

3) Merton Bernstein and Joan Brodshaug-Bernstein, *Social Security: The System That Works* (New York: Basic Books, 1988), 10; Theodore Marmor, Jerry Mashaw and Philip Harvey, *America's Misunderstood Welfare State: Persistent Myths, Enduring Realities* (New York: Basic Books, 1990), 46; and Arthur M Schlesinger, *The Coming of the New Deal, Vol. 3 of The Age of Roosevelt* (Cambridge: Houghton Mifflin Company, 1958), 301-303.

4) Leuchtenburg, 103-4.

5) Schlesinger, 304; Mamor, Mashaw and Harvey, 33-34; Edward Berkowitz, *America's Welfare State: From Roosevelt to Reagan* (Baltimore: Johns Hopkins University Press, 1991), 15, 191; Social Security Administration, *A Brief History of Social Security.* (Washington, D.C.: U.S. Government Printing Office, SSA Publication No. 21-059, 1995), 2. (*A Brief History of Social Security* hereinafter is referred to as *ABHOSS*.)

6) Mamor, Mashaw and Harvey, 33-4; Committee on Economic Security, *Report to the President* (Washington, D.C.: U.S. Government Printing Office, 1935), 20-41.

7) Berkowitz, 20-21; Douglas, 75-6.

8) Leuchtenburg, 165-166; Berkowitz, 25.

9) Schlesinger, 306-309; Leuchtenburg, 130-132; Mamor, Mashaw and Harvey, 33-34; Berkowitz, ix.

10) Leuchtenburg, 145-147, 130-132, 150, 237; Schlesinger, 311-2; Berkowitz, 15 and 191.

11) Leuchtenburg, 145-147, 130-132, 150, 237; Schlesinger, 311-312; Berkowitz 15 and191; Joseph Martin, *My First Fifty Years in Politics* (New York: McGraw Hill, 1960), 66-7, 74, 117; Douglas, 101

12) Leuchtenburg, 132-133; *ABHOSS*, 8-10; United States, Congress. *Compilation of the Social Security Laws, Including the Social Security Act, as Amended, and Related Enactments.* Public Law 74-271. (Washington, D.C.: U.S. Government Printing Office, 1999); Berkowitz 25. (*Compilation of the Social Security Laws....*hereinafter referred to as *PL 74-271*)

13) Schlesinger, 306-309; Leuchtenburg, 130-132; Mamor, Mashaw and Harvey, 33-34.

14) Berkowitz, 14, 190; Schlesinger, 311-312; Leuchtenburg, 132-133; *ABHOSS*, 8-10; PL 74-271.

15) Leuchtenburg, 131, 252; Schlesinger, 312-313; Martin, 66-67, 74, 117; Douglas, 101-2; Paul Boller, Jr, *Congressional Anecdotes* (New York: Oxford University Press, 1991), 240-3; William A. DeGregorio, *The Complete Book of U.S. Presidents* (New York: Barricade Books, 1991), 504.

16) Leuchtenburg, 273-4.

17) Leuchtenburg, 237, 273-4, 347; Douglas, 68.

18) Berkowitz, 28.

19) Leuchtenburg, 274.

20) Leuchtenburg, 132-133; *ABHOSS*, 8-10; *PL 74-271*; Berkowitz, 39-40, 191; Bernstein, 10.

21) Douglas, 386-7.

22) Leuchtenburg, 320, 322.

23) Berkowitz, 14, 190.

24) Sheri David, "Eisenhower and the American Medical Association: A Coalition Against the Elderly," in *Dwight D Eisenhower: Soldier, President, Statesman,* ed. Joann Krieg (New York: Greenwood Press, 1987), 57; Schlesinger, 311-315; Leuchtenburg, 320.

25) Berkowitz, 159.

26) Berkowitz, 164.

27) Berkowitz, 164-5.

28) Berkowitz, 165.

29) Berkowitz, 39-40, 191; Bernstein 12, 26, 187, 214-215.

CHAPTER TWO

Eisenhower's Initial Success

In 1953, the average American had little contact with Social Security unless he or she had been widowed or retired. Few understood the program's details, scope, fiscal condition or legal rules. The meaning of Social Security to many younger workers was restricted to the FICA deduction on their weekly payroll stubs and the distant thought of retirement. Destitution among aged Americans was becoming less common as Social Security increasingly separated old age from poverty. The alternative of retiring on a pension was becoming more viable as opposed to working until one fell over dead or suffered a severe illness or injury. Pension plans were increasingly common in blue and white-collar industries. Seniors were able to retire comfortably on their employer pensions, so long as they were supplemented by Social Security. This generated widespread support for Social Security and Americans were willing to pay higher tax rates rather than have the program cut. All of this was fine for older Americans who had not suffered a disabling illness or injury over the course of their careers. The problem, however, was that the existing system worked only for those who managed to retain their good health from their teens into their sixties.[1]

Following the end of World War II, the United States had become a world economic power whose powerful economy supported unprecedented levels of prosperity. Many Americans, for the first time, experienced economic comfort, but the wealth was not shared equally and some did not reap any rewards at all. Tax collections for the Social Security Trust Fund annually exceeded outgoing payments and the trust fund grew accordingly. The glaring omission in all this prosperity and reform was social insurance coverage for disabled persons. A wage earner that suffered a disability was a greater financial burden to his family than if he had simply died. In both instances, the family would suffer a loss of income, but death is one-time expense. A wage earner's disability would continue to drain the family's resources through ongoing medical expenses.[2]

Dwight D Eisenhower became President of the United States in January 1953. By nature, he was not a casual man. There was nothing accidental about him; he never acted without a plan. In conducting his affairs, whether as a military officer or as President of the United States, he always wanted to maintain control. By the time he became President, he had had a long career as a high ranking military officer. He was acutely aware of his place in the order of things as the first Republican president in twenty years. Eisenhower knew exactly what he wanted to accomplish in proposing amendments to the Social Security Act, but he found it difficult to convert his ideas into practice. A president is as much a politician as any small town legislator, but Eisenhower despised politics. Accustomed to deference, he found it lacking in legislators. Eisenhower had trouble organizing his party, his advisors and the White House staff. Unlike Franklin Roosevelt, Eisenhower could not wear the presidency like a comfortable suit. He had to learn how to be President, just like Harry Truman before him.[3]

This did not mean that Eisenhower was a stranger to politics nor the arts of negotiation and compromise. His reputation to this point was built largely on his ability to reconcile diverging viewpoints, as ably demonstrated by his success in commanding the Allied forces in Europe in the Second World War. These skills did not desert him in the White House. Eisenhower saw himself as very different from Truman. Eisenhower believed that he possessed an important leadership quality that Truman lacked—the ability to inspire Americans to have faith in the office of the president. For all his successes, Truman never substantially enjoyed the confidence of the people. Eisenhower believed that he had a mandate for change. The timing of his election was perfect as he was now in a position to build on the New and Fair Deals while putting a stop to runaway spending. Like the Republicans of the 1930's, Eisenhower wanted to control the excesses of "big government." But he accepted more of the New and Fair Deals than those Republicans of the Depression Era did. In this effort, he was very selective. He believed in a limited role for the federal government, but advocated a few massive federally financed projects of his own. For example, he was a proponent of the Interstate Highway System, free distribution of the polio vaccine, expanded public housing, national health insurance and federal aid for the construction of new hospitals and schools. Social Security was one of the New Deal programs that he wanted to expand.[4]

The mood of America at the time of Eisenhower's election was that it had had enough social reform. Since Reconstruction, Presidents had had little success in forcing unpopular plans on the public. Wilson had failed with the League of Nations, FDR in packing the Supreme Court and Truman with national health insurance. Eisenhower cast himself as a figure of conciliation and paternalism even as his detractors believed that he lacked the proper skills to succeed as a politician. Eisenhower used this perception to his advantage when he complained about the failure of the "politicians" to cooperate with his efforts. He carefully cultivated the image of a moral leader defending standards of decency and the status quo. His method was to convince rather than coerce, charm rather than threaten. Above all, he displayed civilized patience.[5]

Eisenhower was personally very conservative concerning social welfare programs. If the Republican Party were to prosper, however, he understood that he would have to temper his private conservatism. Eisenhower also understood that any attempt to cut or eliminate the Social Security program was political suicide. While most Americans were content with the status of the Social Security program, pressure was mounting from the working class to address the needs of the disabled. Eisenhower sought to reap the political benefits by leading the charge. His personal charisma and his Republican social programs would wrest the support of the common man away from the Democrats. He emphasized that, "The Republican Party yields to no one its concern for the human needs of human beings."[6] This would become the basis of his "Dynamic Conservatism." However, as far as Social Security was concerned, the 1952 Republican Party Platform called only for reducing the number of non-covered professions for retirement and survivor benefits. It made no mention of entitlement for the disabled.[7]

Eisenhower saw his policy of Dynamic Conservatism as the guiding principle of his presidency. Eric F Goldman recounted some clarifying remarks made by the President in 1954. Eisenhower emphasized that the administration

> must be liberal when it was talking about the relationship between the Government and the individual, conservative when talking about the national economy and the individual's pocketbook.[8]

Eisenhower wanted to preserve the gains of the New and Fair Deals. He believed that the Republican Party could shake its image of being the party of Big Business by pursuing its own agenda of moderate social welfare programs while thwarting more radical Democratic alternatives. To this end, he was careful to reassure a wary public that he had accepted the social gains of the last twenty years as a solid foundation through which the welfare of all individuals could be protected. Some extensions would be advocated but for the most part not vigorously pressed, and the whole was to be set within a severe budget consciousness. Adlai Stevenson, twice Eisenhower's electoral opponent for the presidency, responded to what sounded to him like nonsense:

I am not even sure what it means when one says that he is a conservative in fiscal affairs and a liberal in human affairs. I assume what it means is that you will strongly recommend the building of a great many schools to accommodate the needs of our children, but not provide the money.[9]

Conservative Republicans did not embrace Dynamic Conservatism. It was too similar to the New and Fair Deal legislation they had been resisting for the last generation. There was a lot of grumbling about how Eisenhower was not in tune with the needs and wants of the Party and that it was a mistake to have elected him president. Despite these misgivings, some conservative legislators saw some advantage in cooperating with Eisenhower. If the President's program failed, they feared the next administration would be Democratic and more to the left. The conservative cause lived or died, they believed, on the success of the Eisenhower administration. After all, his program was a moderate one and a record that did not appeal to the voters at the next election would mean dire consequences for Republicans in general.[10]

The Eisenhower administration believed that the well being of corporate enterprise was essential to the well being of the nation. Eisenhower saw the international and domestic imperatives for building the United States into an even greater industrial power. It was warfare in the economic rather than conventional sense. Secretary of Defense Charles Wilson once remarked, "What's good for General Motors is good for the United States." However, in the course of expanding industrialization, there would be casualties. Men and women, in some instances, would pay for this economic advancement with their health and earnings potential. Disabled workers were becoming an increasing concern. It was on the backs of these people that the nation prospered, and it was wrong to cast them aside after their sacrifice. Just as soldiers were the casualties of conventional conflict, the disabled were the casualties of industry. Eisenhower knew war and he hated it. He was determined to find some way to assist these disabled people without betraying his principles. He initially thought that protection against events beyond an individual's control could be provided through the federal government in coordination with privately sponsored plans. But, like Franklin Roosevelt before him, Eisenhower found little support for national reinsurance plans. Still, the solution did not lie in enacting new legislation. Eisenhower believed that enough social legislation had been enacted since 1933. He wanted to refine what already existed to make it more efficient, fiscally and bureaucratically, rather than dismantle it. He made it clear to his cabinet and other advisors that the federal government had a responsibility for the welfare of the people.[11]

Eisenhower wanted to protect the pension rights of those disabled at a young age and he wanted them to receive assistance so that they could once again become productive members of the work force. He did not advocate a federally funded program for monetary payments to disabled workers; rather, he envisioned a federal program of vocational rehabilitation that recycled a valuable resource: the American worker. Just because a disability prevented a worker from performing at one job did not mean that he or she could not learn another vocation. Such a program did not encourage sloth or perpetuate a vicious cycle of dependency upon government handouts. It was economically viable because the economy drew strength from productive wage earners while those on the public dole were a hindered economic progress.

President Eisenhower wanted to proceed incrementally in amending the Social Security Act in order to maintain control. He wanted only his agenda to be enacted and only to the extent that he desired. He did not want his program to be co-opted into something that was at odds with his principles. He believed that the key to this endeavor was to have the officials serving under him engaged in a unified effort. To guard against dissent, Eisenhower deliberately organized the bureaucracy of his White House to reflect that of the United States Army, believing from personal experience that the Army was the most efficiently run bureaucracy in the world. The core of this White House bureaucracy was the President's cabinet.[12]

At the expense of some of his political capital, Eisenhower chose his cabinet with the singular focus that it would conduct itself in an efficient, businesslike manner. Ultimately, critics charged that the cabinet was comprised of the overly affluent, insulating the President from the concerns of average citizens. Eisenhower did not like this corporate identity that was being forced upon his administration. The justification for his selections was that politicians had been running the government since 1932. He believed it was necessary now for businessmen to take over in order to restore the confidence of the American people in their government and their president. Eisenhower had tried to remove the stigma of "partisan politics as usual" by touting himself as the apolitical man. He made it a point to remind Republicans not to favor big business at the expense of the ordinary person. Eisenhower's plan to amend the Social Security Act was a program of vocational rehabilitation intended to appeal to both worker and owner by providing assistance to the common man without increasing the tax burden on the business community.[13]

Eisenhower publicly downplayed his role in the decision-making process as president, thus shielding himself from criticism. To this end, he refrained from making specific, personal attacks and avoided flaunting his power. He had a violent temper, but never displayed it in public. He allowed himself to be perceived as susceptible to the influence of Chief of Staff Sherman Adams, Secretary of State John Foster Dulles and others so that legislators and the general public would blame his subordinates for any disagreements. This strategy enabled him to avoid the hostility and anger of his detractors and made Eisenhower a much more likeable figure. His use of "hidden-hand" tactics paid the immediate dividend of allowing him to remain cordial with his political enemies. The drawback was that at times he appeared indecisive and unable to take charge of a situation. His style of remaining on the periphery sacrificed some of the power and prestige of the office of the president and it led to some unnecessarily protracted struggles. The press underplayed Eisenhower's role in the administration, following the president's lead, and some mistakenly concluded that he was above politics or that he did not understand policy. This was far from the truth. Publicly he advocated a strict separation of powers, that the President should propose and the Congress dispose. In reality, Eisenhower actively pursued his legislative agenda through public persuasion and private negotiation.[14]

Eisenhower did not get along as easily with politicians as Roosevelt and Truman did, so he preferred to deal with Congress through his subordinates. However, legislators did not like being told what to do, especially by non-elected bureaucrats, and they felt were entitled to speak directly to the President from time to time. While the President was the head of the party and the head of the government, and entitled to the respect and consideration those positions brought, it was also his responsibility to afford the same courtesies to Congressmen. Eisenhower's failure to do so fostered a sometimes-contentious relationship between the Republican legislators and the President. Again, criticism was not directed against him; his assistants, primarily Sherman Adams, bore the brunt of any ill will.[15]

Eisenhower interpreted the Constitution very narrowly in defining his role in domestic affairs. In contrast to Roosevelt and Truman, who had blurred the lines, Eisenhower believed in a formal separation of authority among the three branches of government. Eisenhower limited himself to proposing legislation on the advice of his cabinet and others; he did not want to lead or cajole congressmen into voting as he desired. He initially left congressional leadership in the hands of Senate Majority Leaders Robert Taft (R-OH), then William Knowland (R-CA), and Speaker of the House Joseph Martin, but this did not produce the desired results. Eisenhower still expected deference and when it was not forthcoming, he was annoyed at having to resort to the normal tactics of a politician, such as persuasion, argument and making deals.[16]

By 1952, the Republican Party had split into two factions, the Old Guard Republicans and the Eisenhower Republicans. The Old Guard included some legislators who had been fighting the uphill battle against the Democrats and the New Deal since the early 1930's. Most were conservatives from the west and mid-west, both young and old, who had never warmed to the New Deal. The Republicans had been the minority party for two decades and these members of the Old Guard were now relishing the opportunity to dismantle the New and Fair Deals. They considered themselves the true Republicans and expected the President to fall into line with them. A significant portion of this faction had opposed Eisenhower's nomination; because he was not a Republican of long-standing. Prominent members of the Old Guard included Senator Robert Taft of Ohio, the Republican leader in the Senate and Eisenhower's former rival for the Republican presidential nomination, William Knowland of California, Taft's successor; and Representative Joseph Martin of Massachusetts, the new Speaker of the House of Representatives.[17]

The Eisenhower Republicans were the group that had supported Eisenhower's nomination and they tended to be those who did not occupy high-ranking positions throughout the 1930's and 1940's. Most were from the east and northeast. This group was not committed to dismantling the New and Fair Deals, but to preserving what was practically viable. This was not a shift toward a more liberal position, but merely an acceptance of the new order of things. This acceptance was lacking in the Old Guard. The Eisenhower Republicans tended to be more moderate than the conservative Old Guard and their critics charged that they sounded too much like Democrats. At the start of the 1952 campaign, Eisenhower had aligned himself with this more moderate faction of the party, comprised of men like Senators Thomas Kuchel of California, John Sherman Cooper of Kentucky, and Representatives Clifford Case of New Jersey and Jacob Javits of New York. Eisenhower further demonstrated his affiliation when, after his election, he pointedly made his cabinet appointments without seeking the counsel of Old Guard Republicans. This demonstrated that he was not going to defer to the likes of Taft or Martin, who believed that protocol demanded that they should have been consulted on cabinet appointments. He responded to this criticism by pointing out that he did not seek the consul of the Eisenhower Republicans, either. The Old

Guard still resented its exclusion from the decision-making process and the loss of opportunities to reward loyal supporters of the Republican Party. This split in the party negated the slim Republican majority in the 83rd Congress, but its effects were lessened by a similar schism in the Democratic Party.[18]

Personally, Eisenhower was skeptical of the federal government's ability to manage any sort of disability or national health care program. The President had seen enough graft and corruption in the military and the Veterans Administration to doubt that any federal agency could operate in the best interests of the disabled if cash benefit payments were involved. Even in the absence of thievery and with the Social Security Administration firmly in place, he imagined any additional programs would only add another layer of bureaucracy that would not, or could not, satisfactorily meet the goals originally intended. It was also well known that private insurance companies had yet to find a way to offer disability insurance at a profit. Should a way be found, Eisenhower did not want to deny the private sector the opportunity for profit. The American Medical Association (AMA) constantly reminded him that it was not the role of the federal government to deny any segment of private industry the potential for profit. Eisenhower concurred and believed that the Social Security system was not a substitute for individual prudence. Private savings, pension plans and other insurance protection should remain as the primary source of insulation against calamity, with Social Security serving as a welcome, but not desperately needed, supplement.[19]

Eisenhower advocated a national reinsurance plan to meet the needs of those who required health insurance or disability protection. He had faith in the private sector and charitable institutions to serve the greater pubic good. He endorsed a bill in his State of the Union Address on February 2, 1953 that he felt was consistent with the aims of the AMA. The President emphasized that each citizen required safeguards against personal disaster in an industrial economy and that the federal government shared some responsibility for this along with the private sector. He called for enhancing, not overhauling, the existing social insurance programs and welfare systems in America. Eisenhower believed that the existing Social Security laws should be extended to cover millions left out of the system, but he also stressed the need for more reliance on private pension plans. This combination of private and public programs, he felt, would "avoid government by bureaucracy as carefully as it avoid[ed] neglect of the helpless."[20]

Despite Eisenhower's endorsement, the reinsurance bill died in committee because the AMA lobbied ardently against it. The AMA would not tolerate any sort of federal interference in the practice of medicine, however tangential. The physicians did not want the medical profession to come under the existing Old Age and Survivor Insurance (OASI) program offered by Social Security. They argued that the additional taxation was a cross physicians did not need or want to bear, and that the medical community did not require federal assistance to plan for retirement. They asserted that any increase in the federal role in the current health care system or in the way that the state-run disability programs were managed would bring America that much closer to socialized medicine. This claim that Social Security would lead to socialized medicine angered Eisenhower, who opposed socialized medicine. He felt that his proposal clearly advocated an improvement in current conditions without raising the specter of the AMA's worst nightmare. The AMA's opposition left the President with no other choice but to look to a government program managed by Social Security.[21]

Eisenhower carefully defined what his objectives were going to be in amending the Social Security Act. Eisenhower wanted to extend coverage to millions of workers who were not covered by the program and he also wanted a disability program of vocational rehabilitation supported by a "freeze" of the worker's earnings record. Vocational rehabilitation meant the federally funded retraining of disabled workers to learn new skills in order to re-enter the workforce at different occupations. "Freezing" a worker's earnings record meant that the worker's retirement benefits would not be adversely affected by the period of months or years that he was involuntarily unable to work.

Initial cabinet discussions in early 1953 were favorable to the President's plans, but there was concern over the Republican response in Congress to the expansion of a New Deal program.[22]

Eisenhower decided to proceed with his plan for Social Security incrementally, to determine with each step what was politically feasible and acceptable to the public. The first step in enacting this program was to consolidate presidential authority over Social Security by creating a new cabinet post. It would play well in the media for Eisenhower to declare that Social Security concerns warranted cabinet level representation. In addition, the proposed legislation would benefit from the support of a cabinet secretary.[23]

A three-member Social Security Board (SSB), formed in August 1935 originally administered the Social Security program. Chairman John Winant, Arthur Altmeyer and Vincent Miles were the initial board members. The chairman of the SSB reported directly to the President. In July 1939, Reorganization Plan No. 1 placed the SSB under the jurisdiction of the Federal Security Agency (FSA), and the SSB chairman then reported to the administrator of the FSA. In July 1946, Reorganization Plan No. 2 abolished the SSB and replaced it with the Social Security Administration (SSA), and Arthur Altmeyer was appointed as the first Commissioner of the SSA. The SSA still reported to the FSA. Eisenhower decided in 1953 that it was time for another change.[24]

The President wanted to make amends with the AMA and also wanted to demonstrate clearly that he was opposed to socialized medicine. At this time, Arthur Altmeyer, a holdover from the Roosevelt and Truman administrations, was still the Commissioner of Social Security. Altmeyer was still loudly advocating Truman's failed plans for national health insurance and calling for the expansion of the Social Security program in general, including disability benefits. Eisenhower wanted to get rid of him, fearing that Altmeyer's impolitic approach would generate animosity toward his own plans.[25]

Eisenhower sent a special message to Congress on March 12, 1953, outlining Reorganization Plan No. 1 of 1953. This plan called for the elimination of the FSA and the creation of a new cabinet level department called Health, Education and Welfare (HEW). HEW would assume organizational jurisdiction for SSA, among other responsibilities. This was essentially the same plan that Truman had submitted in 1950. Truman's proposal was rejected because Republicans, conservative Democrats and the AMA all mistrusted FSA Administrator Oscar Ewing, an ardent Fair Dealer, and the man who would have ascended to the post of cabinet secretary. Opponents feared that Truman and Ewing would conspire to enact a socialized health plan. However, Eisenhower had a strong reputation of opposing any federal expansion and anything socialist in nature. His word was sufficient to assuage any doubts by the legislators.[26]

In his special message, Eisenhower explained that he wanted vital health, education and Social Security matters to be carried out by a cabinet level official because he believed this was consistent with the "importance and magnitude" of the issues involved. He called for an unremitting effort to improve social programs that have proven their effectiveness and asserted that a cabinet level official would best serve this need. Under this plan, the Commissioner of Social Security would require Senate confirmation. Given the composition and mood of Congress on national health insurance issues, this meant that Altmeyer was out.[27]

Eisenhower intended to appoint Oveta Culp Hobby, the current head of the FSA, as the first Secretary of HEW. Hobby was the spouse of the publisher of the *Houston Post* and its former editor, and a prominent Democrat for Eisenhower in the 1952 election. She had earned a reputation as a competent administrator as the head of the FSA under President Truman and during the first three months of the Eisenhower Administration. She also had had an amicable relationship with Eisenhower during her tenure as commander of the Women's Army Corps (WAC) in the Second World War. The President had every expectation that HEW, as run by Hobby, could efficiently serve the needs of the American people. Her independent Texas background would add a southern and bipartisan element to the cabinet. Hobby was reluctant initially to accept the position, but soon consented after some urging by Eisenhower. She believed personally in the Social Security program and in Eisenhower's perception of its role in American society. She formally took office on April 11, 1953.[28]

Eisenhower learned from his mistake with the State of the Union address and made sure to pay his respects to the AMA. On March 14, 1953, accompanied by Secretary-to-be Hobby, he addressed the House of Delegates of the American Medical Association at the Statler Hotel in Washington. In his remarks, the President declared that the government could do more for national health if it cooperated with the doctors instead of trying to force itself upon them. Eisenhower allayed the concerns of his audience by being blunt:

> I have certain philosophical bonds with doctors. I don't like the word "compulsory." I am against the word "socialized"....(We will not) forsake our traditional system of free enterprise....That is the doctrine of the Administration.[29]

By agreeing not to pursue a national health insurance plan, and promising that Altmeyer would be removed, Eisenhower ensured that the AMA would not stand in the way of the creation of HEW. The AMA's House of Delegates unanimously endorsed his plan. On April 11, 1953, FSA was formally abolished and replaced by the Department of HEW. The former FSA Administrator, Oveta Culp Hobby, was appointed as HEW's first Secretary. The Commissioner of SSA now reported directly to Hobby. She immediately reassured the AMA that she would look out for its best interests, i.e. minimal government interference in the practice of medicine and no national public health insurance system for the sick and elderly, if she could count on their cooperation in other administration objectives.[30]

Hobby's views on Social Security were compatible with Eisenhower's. From May 1953 through July 1953, under the supervision of the President, Hobby prepared for congressional consideration the next legislative proposals to amend the Social Security Act. The

President and the Secretary agreed that the extension of OASI should not be tied to disability. The extension of OASI, a modification of the existing law, was going to be difficult enough without the added complications disability invited. They also agreed that in order to maintain the low overhead cost of the OASI program, ensure the continued solvency of the trust fund and increase the spending power of older Americans, additional workers were needed to contribute to the program. Eisenhower submitted a proposal for the extension OASI coverage to the House Committee on Ways and Means in a special message transmitted August 1, 1953. The President emphasized that Social Security, in its current form, was an essential part of American economic and social life, but that there was an urgent need for refining the program to make it more effective. He claimed that:

> These systems are but a reflection of the American heritage of sturdy self reliance which has made our country strong and kept it free [and eager] to push to ever widening horizons in every aspect of our national life."[31]

He assured the legislators that the proposals had been thoroughly reviewed not only by the Department of HEW, but also by the Secretary herself. Hobby and the President had concluded that an extension of Social Security was needed in the same fashion that had been outlined in the State of the Union Address back in February. Eisenhower proposed extending Social Security coverage to self-employed farmers, farm workers, domestic workers, doctors, dentists, lawyers, architects, accountants and other white collar professionals. State and local municipal workers were offered the option of joining the program. It was estimated that this would bring an additional 10 million workers under Social Security. The President stressed his faith in the principles of the OASI program, which, he asserted, was essential to the continued growth of the national economy. "We must not only preserve this systematic practice, but extend it at every desirable opportunity," Eisenhower declared. "We now have both such an opportunity and a definite plan."[32] The President also noted that "other important improvements" in the Social Security Act were currently under study and would be the subject of further recommendations. An attached memorandum from Hobby outlined the breakdown of the new categories of coverage.[33]

At this point, Eisenhower's efforts at enacting legislation were somewhat clumsy; he expected deference to his wishes and was still learning how to exercise his authority as President. In the 83rd Congress, the Republicans had a one-seat advantage in the Senate and a ten-seat advantage in the House. The struggle with the Old Guard for control of the Republican Party was ongoing and had divided the party, essentially eliminating the advantage of numbers. The ideological ambiguity of many of Eisenhower's programs resulted in a less than cohesive effort on the part of the Republicans. This was a reflection of the split within the party. Eisenhower was forced to build bipartisan coalitions, something he was not skilled at doing. House Democratic Leader Sam Rayburn's (D-TX) growing irritation at repeatedly being used as a crutch added to Eisenhower's ineffectiveness. The August 1, 1953 proposal for changes to the Social Security Act died through legislative inertia in the House Committee on Ways and Means. The Old Guard Republicans resisted not simply because they opposed the expansion of New Deal programs, but because they did not want to levy additional taxes for the purposes of retirement, which they believed should largely remain a personal matter. Daniel Reed (R-NY), Chairman of the House Committee on Ways and Means, believed that the administration's proposal was a "patchwork job" and required further study. The legislation was allowed to die quietly through parliamentary procedure. Rebuking and then alienating the President was not smart politics.[34]

Frustrated, but undaunted, Eisenhower considered a new approach. He gave Secretary Hobby the responsibility of devising a new proposal. More thought was given to the content of the bill and the strategy that would be used to steer it through Congress. Eisenhower realized that he could not demand passage of this legislation and that OASI was too complicated to be evaluated in general terms.

In a cabinet meeting on November 20, 1953, Secretary Hobby unveiled her proposal to expand the Social Security program. Under her plan, the system would remain a contributory system and benefit payments would continue to be related, in part, to individual earnings. Secretary of Labor James Mitchell suggested abandoning the fixed age requirement for retirement benefits. He reasoned that age 65 had been unjustly stigmatized as an age for forced retirement. Undersecretary of the Treasury Marion Folsom agreed with Hobby that the fixed age requirement was essential to the success of the program. The basis for Social Security benefit computations was not work credit and FICA tax contributions alone; the beneficiary's age and date of filing were the primary components of the benefit formula. To alter the fixed age requirement would require an overhaul of the existing system. Hobby, and most importantly the President, only wanted to expand the program as it existed, not reinvent it. It was not the mission of Social Security to tilt at the windmills of age discrimination.[35]

Eisenhower reported that Senator Taft (who had died on July 31, 1953) had advocated that everyone should get paid at age 65 to reduce administrative complications to the program. Secretary of the Treasury George Humphrey used this opening to bring up the proposal of Congressmen Daniel Reed (R-NY) and Carl Curtis (R-NE). The Reed-Curtis plan called for the payment of retirement benefits for everyone who reached 65, regardless of work histories, and financing the program on a pay-as-you-go basis. Reed-Curtis had been considered by Congress back in March and April 1953 and the legislators as a whole had simply hated it, calling it a criminal raid on the trust fund surplus accumulated by worker contributions. Eisenhower did not reject the proposal outright; rather, he turned it over to Hobby for further study. Hobby was aware of the Reed-Curtis plan and stated diplomatically that her proposal was more attractive politically. Director of Foreign Operations Harold Stassen urged Eisenhower to act quickly to support Hobby's proposal; the prestige of a presidential endorsement would undercut any lingering congressional support for Reed-Curtis, thus avoiding a protracted struggle over competing bills. The Undersecretary of HEW, Nelson Rockefeller, warned Hobby that her proposal could be sabotaged if its details were revealed outside the Cabinet prematurely, given the mood of Congress and its committee leaders. Men like William Knowland, Walter George (D-GA) and Wilbur Mills would be opposed to the expansion of any surviving New Deal programs. After Hobby summarized her program as economically sound, the Cabinet and the President broke into applause, essentially approving Hobby's proposals for Social Security reform.[36]

Eisenhower ended the cabinet meeting with a vigorous statement emphasizing the need to enact a moderate, progressive social program. He believed that preserving many of the social reforms of the 1930's was a necessity, not only to steal the thunder of the Democrats, but to ensure the continued progress of American society. The way to accomplish this was to modernize and strengthen programs that had demonstrated longevity of relevance, only one of which was Social Security. He followed his own inclination to revise what existed rather than to alter radically. This would seem to be in conflict with the disability "freeze" and vocational rehabilitation components of the bill, innovations that went far beyond simple revisions of the existing law. Eisenhower justified these provisions by citing the failure of the private sector to address the very real needs of the disabled worker, and stressed that they did not compromise the American value system of self-reliance. The sick and the injured would be retrained and returned to work once again to earn their own living as opposed to creating a new dependent underclass scraping by on the federal dole.[37]

Eisenhower and Hobby spent much of their time in December 1953 cultivating support for the new Social Security proposals. The President even appealed directly for public support in a radio and TV address on January 4, 1954. Eisenhower acknowledged that the federal government bore some of the responsibility for the welfare of its citizens, and noted that he had recommended an expansion of Social

Security coverage in 1953 that was designed to save workers from destitution in the event of personal disaster. He also explained that a greater role for Social Security would reduce federal grants in aid to local welfare programs. He told the American people that he expected congressional action on these issues in 1954.[38]

Finally, on January 14, 1954, Eisenhower played his hand. In a special message to Congress, he submitted his proposal to the House Committee on Ways and Means. Eisenhower asserted that his proposal would reduce "both the fear and the incidence of destitution to a minimum (and) to promote the confidence of every individual in the future. These are proper aims of all levels of government, including the Federal Government."[39] Private savings, investment, insurance and a healthy economy were the primary means of protection against the hazards of old age and an untimely death or disability. The sound tax and fiscal policies of the government would ensure that such options always existed. However, Social Security was also prudent in that it could be used as a base to build upon. The worker used his earnings from his most productive years to protect his economic standing in the case of calamity, or a higher standard of living in planned retirement. Eisenhower emphasized that "a basic, nationwide protection against these hazards can be provided through a government social insurance system."[40]

Eisenhower's proposal, designated now as H.R. 7199, specifically proposed extending OASI coverage recommended along the lines he had advocated in August; liberalizing the retirement test from $75 per month to $1,000 per annum; instituting cost of living adjustments (COLA); increasing the taxable earnings base from $3,000 to $3600; and computing benefits in a new way which would result in higher benefit payments. Eisenhower also called for the creation of a disability program with dual elements: a "freeze" and vocational rehabilitation. With a disability "freeze," a person's retirement benefit computation would not be adversely affected by the large number of "zero earnings years" on his or her earnings record if the SSA determined that the person was disabled and could not work. Those years would become "drop out years" and would not be used in the computation to determine the worker's monthly benefit amount payable upon reaching retirement age. The worker's earnings record was considered "frozen" because the worker was outside the work force due to circumstances beyond his or her control. In conjunction with "freeze," if the SSA found a worker to be disabled and unable to work, but possessing the skills or the ability to learn other skills to return to work in a different capacity, he or she would qualify for a federally funded program of vocational rehabilitation. The vocational rehabilitation programs would be run by the states because they were seen as more responsive to local job markets and already had the bureaucratic apparatuses in place as a result of their own state-run disability programs. Eisenhower stated that the projected cost of the disability program was one-half of one percent of all the annual FICA tax revenues.[41]

Labor unions were ecstatic about the Eisenhower administration's proposal. From their view, this bill demonstrated once and for all that Social Security was not charity and that retirement benefits were an earned right. George Meany, president of the American Federation of Labor (AFL), was optimistically cautious:

> The Administration's proposals represent as forward looking a program as the Administration has yet produced. They repudiate the irresponsible efforts that have been made by....others to undermine the structure of the social insurance system. The AFL welcomes the President's recommendations as a long step forward in preserving, improving and extending the American Social Security system.[42]

A few days later, Eisenhower further clarified the program of vocational rehabilitation, which was intended to restore the more than two million handicapped Americans to work. The President reported that 250,000 were disabled annually and that the existing system only returned 60,000 annually to productive work. Eisenhower wanted to reverse this alarming trend. This change made economic sense as the

United States spent three times as much in public assistance to care for the non-productive disabled as it would cost to rehabilitate them into self sufficient tax-paying workers. Once rehabilitated, they would pay back the cost of their rehabilitation through taxation multi-fold. Eisenhower recommended appropriating funds to construct new hospitals and medical facilities to assist the disabled. Such modern facilities and the inherent commitment in the medical profession to assist the disadvantaged, he argued, would attract the best physicians to the program.[43]

Complementing this program of vocational rehabilitation would be a national reinsurance health plan. Eisenhower urged for Congress to set aside $25 million in a trust fund to establish a federal reinsurance service to encourage private and non profit health insurance providers to offer broader protection to more families. The President emphasized that the proposed program would be vigorous, imaginative and would avoid governmental regimentation of medicine. He used these phrases deliberately to contrast himself to Truman and his failed program. The reinsurance plan was generally well received by Congress, but Senator Herbert Lehman (D-NY) voiced his doubts, calling the proposal progressive, but vague in key details. The AMA declined to comment on the proposal.[44]

The House Committee on Ways and Means met on January 14, 1954, and Chairman Reed introduced H.R. 7199 immediately upon its receipt from the President. Reed supported the bill, as it was consistent with his own belief that coverage under Social Security should be expanded. In backing the President's bill, Reed effectively abandoned Representative Curtis and their previous approach. The enthusiasm in and out of Congress surrounding the President's bill undercut any support that Curtis had hoped to generate for his plan.[45]

On April 1, 1954, the Ways and Means Committee began public hearings on H.R. 7199. Chairman Reed began the proceedings by reminding everyone that he had introduced the bill, and he emphasized that "this legislation is of vital importance to millions of Americans."[46] Secretary Hobby testified amicably in favor of the bill, citing many statistics to demonstrate the amount of planning that had gone into the President's proposal. She quoted the President as saying that H.R. 7199 was the "cornerstone of the Government's programs to promote the economic security of the individual."[47] HEW's research, she stated, had discovered that Social Security excluded too many occupations for the program to remain solvent and that the current categories of entitlement were inadequate and inequitable. H.R. 7199, she emphasized, would rectify these inequities.[48]

Accompanying Hobby's testimony was that of Undersecretary of HEW Nelson Rockefeller, Assistant Secretary of HEW Roswell Perkins, Director of the Bureau of Old Age and Survivor Insurance Victor Christgau and SSA's Chief Actuary, Robert Myers. Other witnesses testified mainly about the extension of coverage to different professional classes. Groups representing public accountants, nurses, clergymen, public employees, insurance companies, small businessmen, and others were heard. The "freeze" and vocational rehabilitation provisions were largely ignored, except by the AMA contingent, which testified against the bill on April 6.[49] Dr. FJL Blasingame outlined the AMA's position, which was that any federal involvement in the field of medicine, no matter how remote or incidental, was the harbinger of socialized medicine. Blasingame asserted that

> [This bill] cannot be appraised solely as an isolated, detached effort to provide some measure of aid to the disabled worker....Every other step in this direction of a compulsory sickness insurance system must be opposed.[50]

George Meany, representing the AFL, testified in favor of the amendments on April 9, welcoming any aid the federal government was willing to give to the working class. Meany stated:

> These coverage proposals are technically and administratively feasible and socially and economically desirable. We

are aware that they do not provide universal coverage....At the same time, it gives those already covered the advantage of some degree of protection against any future lowering of the average monthly wage because of periods of unemployment, disability or reduced earnings. We urge the adoption of this provision.[51]

Eisenhower was anxious that Congress act on the bill. He was concerned that H.R. 7199 would be greeted with the same apathy as the proposal he had made in 1953. He believed that the legislators were consumed only with getting re-elected at the expense of the general welfare of the nation. James Hagerty, Eisenhower's Press Secretary, recorded in his diary in May 1954 the President's lament:

How they fail to see that the best way they can get re-elected is by supporting the liberal program we have submitted to them is beyond me. If they don't pass a major section of this program, a lot of them, I am sure, are not coming back.[52]

The House Committee on Ways and Means met in executive sessions to consider H.R. 7199 from May 17, 1954 until May 28, 1954. There was a great deal of conflict over which types of workers would be covered under Social Security and which would be excluded. However, there was little controversy over the disability provisions of the bill and they remained unchanged. H.R. 7199 was reported favorably to the House of Representatives on May 28, 1954, but there was still some contention over which amendments to the bill the House would consider. The bill was sent to the House Committee on Rules on June 1, 1954. The Rules Committee immediately issued a closed rule, meaning that only amendments offered by members of the Committee on Ways and Means would be considered. Representative Charles Halleck (R-IN) explained that Social Security was a complex program and that the finer points should not be reconsidered on the House floor; the expertise and judgment of the Committee on Ways and

Means should be accepted. The bill was re-designated H.R. 9366 and then debated by the House of Representatives.[53]

The debate in the House was not acrimonious. Those who voted against the bill, such as Clare Hoffman (R-MI), Edward Robeson (D-VA) and Wint Smith (R-KS), did not take part in the debate or make an entry into the formal record. Chairman Reed and Representative Ray Madden (D-IN) praised the bill without reservation, believing it would bring about more security for the American family and that the prosperity it ensured would be an effective weapon against the influence of Communism. They argued that the changes could be enacted while maintaining the actuarial soundness of the program.[54] Representative Homer Angell (D-OR) voted in favor of the bill, but believed that it still left too many without protection. He commended the President for the ideal behind the bill, but considered it "wholly insufficient"[55] to maintain an acceptable standard of living for the disabled and the elderly. Representative Howard Smith (D-VA) replied that improving the Social Security program was a gradual process and the public needed time to attain a greater understanding of the program in order to ensure future amendments. Smith also warned that it was dangerous to make sweeping changes based upon expectations. Changes should be made to address needs as they occurred, not what they were expected to be. Smith, like Angell, was irked by the closed rule preventing new amendments. They both believed that the bill should be debated at length, not for just one day. Despite some misgivings, most Representatives were satisfied with the bill as a whole, and the measure passed the House on June 1, 1954 by a vote of 356 to 8. It then went to the Senate for consideration.[56]

The Senate Finance Committee began hearings on H.R. 9366 on June 24, 1954. Secretary Hobby testified that the bill passed by the House accurately reflected the President's desires. George Meany testified in favor of the bill, urging that a cash disability program be enacted as well. The AMA contingent testified on July 6, but this time in greater numbers. Dr. Blasingame reiterated his opposition to the proposal, and five other doctors representing different disciplines also testified against the bill, beating the drum of socialized medicine. The Committee continued hearings on the bill through July 9, 1954 and met in executive sessions through July 20. As was the case in the House, the primary disagreement was over which types of workers would be covered or non-covered for OASI purposes. Again, there was minimal controversy over the disability provisions of the bill, which remained unaltered.[57]

In addition to the struggle over H.R. 9366, Eisenhower was still seeking legislative approval of the reinsurance program he had proposed in January 1954. This proposal called for a trust fund to reinsure private voluntary health insurance plans against "abnormal losses." The AMA continued to oppose both health insurance and Social Security reform, effectively raising the specter of socialized medicine. The President's Health Reinsurance Plan of 1954 was facing stiff opposition from the AMA lobby. By July 14, 1954, it seemed certain that the health insurance bill would be defeated. Eisenhower called a meeting of congressional leaders and told them of his disappointment. House Majority Leader Charles Halleck explained that the Democrats were solidly against the bill and that mid-western congressmen had aligned themselves with the wealthy private insurance companies opposed to the measure. Adding the AMA to the mix, prospects were indeed bleak. The President could not fathom the opposition to the bill. He replied to Halleck,

> How in the Hell is the American Medical Association going to stop socialized medicine if they oppose such bills as this. I don't believe the people of the United States are going to stand for being deprived of the opportunity to get medical insurance. If they don't get a bill like this, they will go for socialized medicine sooner or later and the Medical Association will have no one to blame but itself.[58]

Through James Hagerty, the President gave instructions to Secretary Hobby to start getting tough with legislators.[59] As Hagerty recorded in his diary,

> The President told me to tell Mrs. Hobby to "get mad" at the legislative meeting on Monday. "You tell Oveta I said to let her Texas temper get the best of her on Monday, and let those fellows have it." When I returned home that evening, I relayed the information to Mrs. Hobby. She laughed and said, "Don't worry. I'll get mad."[60]

Congressional leaders met with Eisenhower and his advisors on July 19, primarily to discuss the Health Reinsurance bill. The limits of Eisenhower's patience were tested when Senate Majority Leader Knowland suggested that the bill not be actively pursued until 1955, as the influence of the AMA was too strong in Congress. The delay would give both Senators and Representatives an opportunity to work on a strategy to deal with the AMA leadership. Eisenhower responded emphatically:

> We said during the campaign that we were against socialized medicine. One of the things we gave to Mrs. Hobby was her assignment to advance a program which would show the people of this nation that the Republican Party was interested in improving our people's health. As far as I'm concerned, the American Medical Association is just plain stupid. This plan of ours would have shown the people how we could improve their health and stay out of socialized medicine.[61]

Secretary Hobby agreed with the President that there was no way they could do business with the top hierarchy of the AMA. She believed that there was a small group of reactionary men in charge who were "dead set against any change." The meeting was ultimately unproductive, as Eisenhower could not prevail upon the Old Guard

Republicans to see things his way. On July 23, 1954, the House defeated the Health Reinsurance bill by a vote of 238 to 134. Eisenhower was bitterly disappointed and vowed not to support any legislator for re-election who had voted against him.[62]

An angry President Eisenhower faced 133 reporters at a press conference on July 24. Usually punctual and jovial at such events, Eisenhower arrived late and was in a decidedly foul mood. He kept reporters waiting for thirty minutes while he shuffled papers at his desk. Asked to comment on the defeat of the health reinsurance plan, the President stared ahead for a moment, his mouth turned sternly down. As he answered, his fist drummed the desk and his voice rose angrily. He indicated that his proposal was the last barrier against socialized medicine:

> I am sure that the people that voted against this bill just don't understand what are the facts of American life. I don't consider that anyone lost yesterday except the American people…this is only a temporary defeat; this thing will be carried forward as long as I am in office.[63]

All that remained of Eisenhower's social insurance initiatives was the Social Security bill, which would be debated in the Senate in a few days. He was confidant the bill would pass, but with the AMA lurking in the background, nothing was certain.[64]

H.R. 9366 was reported favorably to the Senate on July 27, 1954. The Senate version of the bill differed from that of the House primarily over retirement test provisions, alien eligibility and extending coverage to federal employees. The Senate debated the bill August 12 and 13, 1954. The only debate was a great deal of hair splitting over which professions would be covered by the OASI program. There was no true opposition to the disability provisions of the bill and Senator Eugene Millikin (R-CO) steered it through the Senate. Millikin read aloud from a letter sent to him by Secretary Hobby explaining that the earnings record "freeze" and the vocational rehabilitation items were complementary and codependent. One could not succeed without the other. Millikin agreed with this assessment. H.R. 9366 passed the Senate August 13 by a unanimous voice vote. On August 16, the House formally disagreed with the Senate version of the bill and agreed to a conference committee.[65]

The Conference Committee on the Social Security bill convened in executive session on August 17, 1954. Members included Senators Walter George (D-GA) and Harry Byrd (D-VA) and Representatives Reed (R-NY), Mitchell Jenkins (R-PA), Richard Simpson (R-PA) and John Dingell (D-MI). On August 20, the committee came to agreement. Compromises were made on the OASI coverage issues, but the disability provisions were accepted as Eisenhower had originally proposed them. Existing state agencies would make disability determinations, relieving HEW of the need to create and organize a new level of bureaucracy. In addition, the state agencies already had established relationships with medical professionals in their communities, which would facilitate the development of medical evidence. As the conference report stated,

> The State agencies will apply the standards developed for evaluating severity of impairments for purposes of the freeze. This will promote equal treatment of all disabled individuals...in all States. The cost to these agencies for their services in making disability determinations will be met out of the Trust Fund.[66]

On August 20, both the House and Senate adopted the Conference Committee Report on H.R. 9366 and the bill was cleared for the jubilant President's signature.[67]

Eisenhower was proud of H.R. 9366. It embodied all of the elements of his Dynamic Conservatism in that it provided an increase in services and protection at a reduced cost to the government. It also marked the first time he had gotten the better of the AMA. Eisenhower signed H.R. 9366 into law on September 1, 1954, while on a fishing trip to

Colorado with former President Herbert Hoover. The bill was one of some sixty bills that he signed that day. PL 83-761 mandated an increase in the monthly benefit rate of at least five dollars, a maximum taxable wage base of $4200 (this would yield higher benefit amounts), an increase in the retirement test limit to $1200 per year and the inclusion of professional white collar workers, adding more than ten million additional workers to the Social Security program. Most importantly, the disability "freeze" and vocational rehabilitation programs were now law. Eisenhower had great hopes for vocational rehabilitation and believed that he had delivered a great boon to those at a tremendous disadvantage. As he stressed in his remarks on the new law,

> it reemphasizes to all the world the great value, which we, in America, place upon the dignity and worth of each individual human being....It is a humanitarian investment of great importance, yet it saves substantial sums of money for both Federal and State governments.[68]

Underlining not only the significance of this legislation, Eisenhower also reminded Americans of the other social programs that his administration and Congress had enacted, showing that he had not forgotten the common man. These included increased funding for the construction of hospitals and nursing homes, federal grants to the states for education, a program for federally funded housing and an extension of unemployment benefits.[69]

The public reaction to PL 83-761 was favorable. The *New York Times* hailed it as "the most significant achievement of the Administration."[70] *U.S. News and World Report* examined the amendments in detail and concluded that

> These dozens of changes…add up to a really new and different system of social insurance. It means far more security now for 135 million people and a more comfortable old age

for millions of retiring workers and their wives in the years ahead.[71]

A very satisfied President Eisenhower now considered his work concerning Social Security disability to be over. He gushed at this success, not only for himself, but for the way he had improved the American standard of living. Federal social programs such as Social Security, the Veterans Administration, the Civil Service Retirement System (CSRS) and block grants in aid to the states for unemployment, workmen's compensation and other pensions, were putting nearly 15 billion dollars annually back into the economy. This large amount of assured income to a once cash strapped segment of the population would take the sting out of future recessions. Eisenhower's principle of the public and private sector working together for the overall good of society had been validated.[72] In a letter to Earl Schaefer of the Boeing Airplane Company, Eisenhower emphasized that

> The productivity of a national economy must, at any given time, support the people then living in that nation....The people from twenty to sixty bear the burden of supporting themselves, and, in addition, support those from birth to twenty years of age, and those from sixty to eighty. The problem is how to get this done without going so far in the direction of socialism that a centralized bureaucracy gains excessive control over the lives of all of us. I personally think there has been far too much loose thinking on this matter.[73]

In his subsequent speeches, Eisenhower never tired of trumpeting how he had brought ten million more workers into the OASI program and how he had provided much needed assistance to the disabled. However, despite Eisenhower's victory, problems still remained. The disability provisions of PL 83-761 only assisted a narrow segment of the disabled population. Eisenhower did not craft the legislation with anyone in mind but blue-collar workers who were injured on the job.

While his intention was to help those with severe physical disabilities, the program did not offer any real assistance to those with crippling injuries or acute mental illness that had no realistic chance of benefiting from vocational rehabilitation. The program also assumed that disabled workers wanted to learn new skills and obtain different jobs, but this was not always the case. Eisenhower did not realize that PL 83-761 was a Pandora's Box from which his own worst nightmare would emerge. As Roosevelt had planted the seed for Eisenhower, Eisenhower had planted the seed for those who would turn his disability program into something he never intended.

References: Chapter Two

1) Mamor, Mashaw and Harvey, 132-133; *U.S. News and World Report*, February 27, 1953, 76-81; March 13, 1953, 88-89; and July 30, 1954, 82-84.

2) Bernstein, 10-12, 26, 187, 214-215.

3) Herbert S. Parmet, *Eisenhower and the American Crusades* (New York: MacMillan Company, 1972), 174-5.

4) Robert Branyon, and Lawrence Larsen, eds. *The Eisenhower Administration, 1953-1961: A Documentary History* (New York: Random House, 1971), 234, 430-1; Stephen Ambrose, *Eisenhower: The President* (New York: Simon and Schuster, 1984), 115, 24-25; Parmet, 167; Gary Reichard, *The Reaffirmation of Republicanism: Eisenhower and the 83rd Congress* (Knoxville: University of Tennessee Press, 1975), 9, 225-6.

5) Parmet, 174-5.

6) David, 59.

7) David, 59; Dwight D. Eisenhower, *The White House Years, Vol. 1, Mandate for Change, 1953-1956* (Garden City NY: Doubleday and Company, 1963); Fred I. Greenstein, *The Hidden Hand Presidency: Eisenhower as Leader* (New York: Basic Books, 1982), 49-52; Donald Johnson and Kirk Porter, eds., *National Party Platforms: 1840-1960* (Urbana: University of Illinois Press, 1961), 503; Reichard, 10.

8) Eric Goldman, *The Crucial Decade—and After: America, 1945-1960* (New York: Random House, 1960), 282-3.

9) Goldman, 282-3.

10) Martin, 229, 232-233; D.B. Hardeman and Donald Bacon, *Rayburn: A Biography* (Houston: Gulf Publishing, 1987), 377.

11) Parmet, 175; Charles Alexander, *Holding the Line: The Eisenhower Era, 1952-1961* (Bloomington: Indiana University Press, 1975), 32-33; Norris Cotton, *In the Senate: Amidst the Conflict and the Turmoil* (New York: Dodd, Mead and Company, 1978), 147.

12) Eisenhower, 134-5.

13) Parmet, 168-9, 173; Martin 229, 232-233; Hardeman and Bacon, 377.

14) Branyan and Larsen, 5-6, 8-10; Parmet, 177-8; Duane Tananbaum, *The Bricker Amendment Controversy: A Test of Eisenhower's Political Leadership* (Ithaca: Cornell University Press , 1988), 78-79, 216-218.

15) Elmo Richardson, *The Presidency of Dwight D Eisenhower* (Lawrence: Regents Press of Kansas, 1979), 35; Martin 227, 233; Douglas 385; Sherman Adams, *First Hand Report: The Story of the Eisenhower Administration* (New York: Harper and Brothers, 1961), 73-6.

16) Ambrose, 160; Alexander, 34-5; Richardson, 45-6; Goldman, 55.

17) Richardson, 45; Reichard, 234-5.

18) Richardson, 45; Parmet, 168-9, 173; Douglas, 247; Reichard, 48-9, 234-5; Adams, 57-8.

19) David, 59; Bernstein, 12, 26, 187, 214-215.

20) Branyan and Larsen, 104; *Public Papers of the President: Eisenhower, 1958.* (Washington, D.C.: U.S. Government Printing Office, 1958), 12-34. (*Public Papers of the President* hereinafter referred to as *Pub Potus*.)

21) David, 57, 59; Richardson, 45-6.

22) Ambrose, 48.

23) Ambrose, 48.

24) *ABHOSS*, 4-10; *PL 74-271*, III

25) *New York Times*, March 13, 1953, 1, 18.

26) *Pub Potus, 1953*, 94; *PL 74-271*, III; *Time Magazine*, March 23, 1953, 21-22; *New York Times*, March 13, 1953, 1,18.

27) *Pub Potus, 1953*, 94-5; *PL 74-271*, III; *New York Times*, March 13, 1953, 1, 18.

28) Eisenhower, 92, 134-135; Ambrose, 24; Alexander, 33; David, 59; Parmet, 76; DeGregorio, 538; Douglas, 385; Adams, 62.

29) *Pub Potus, 1953*, 98.

30) David, 59; *ABHOSS*, 10, 31; *PL 74-271*, III; *Time Magazine*, March 23, 1953, 22.

31) *Pub Potus, 1953*, 534.

32) *Pub Potus, 1953*, 535.

33) *Pub Potus, 1953*, 534-6; Eisenhower, 295; *New York Times*, August 2, 1953, 1, 48; U.S., Congress, House of Representatives, Committee on Ways and Means, *Social Security*, House Document 225, 83rd Congress 1st Session, 1953.

34) Eisenhower, 295; Reichard, 49, 119-120, 129-30.

35) Robert Donovan, *Eisenhower: The Inside Story* (New York: Harper and Brothers, 1956), 172-3.

36) Donovan, 172-3.

37) Donovan, 174, 228.

38) Branyan and Larsen, 226; *Pub Potus, 1954*, 2-6.

39) *Pub Potus, 1954*, 62.

40) *Pub Potus, 1954*, 62-68; *New York Times*, January 15, 1954, 1, 11.

41) *Pub Potus, 1954*, 62-68; *New York Times*, January 15, 1954, 1, 11; Reichard, 131-132.

42) *New York Times*, January 15, 1954, 1, 11.

43) *Pub Potus, 1954*, 62-68; *New York Times*, January 19, 1954, 1, 16.

44) *New York Times*, January 19, 1954, 1, 16; Reichard, 133.

45) U.S., Congress, *Congressional Record—Daily Digest,* 83rd Congress, 2nd Session, Volume 100, Part 14, 1954, D18; *New York Times*, January 15, 1954, 11.

    (*Congressional Record—Daily Digest*, herein after referred to as CD)

46) *100 CD (1954)*, D252.

47) U.S., Congress, House of Representatives, Committee on Ways and Means, *Social Security Act Amendments of 1954: Hearings on H.R. 7199*, 83rd Congress, 2nd Session, 1954, 30.

48) *Hearings on H.R. 7199*, 30-35.

49) 100 *CD* (1954), D258, D262, D268, D273, D277-8, D282, D286, D288, D294; *Hearings on H.R. 7199*, 226-231, 450-453.

50) *Hearings on H.R. 7199*, 227-228.

51) *Hearings on H.R. 7199*, 452-453.

52) Robert Ferrell, ed., *The Diary of James C Hagerty: Eisenhower in Mid-Course, 1954-1955* (Bloomington: Indiana University Press, 1983), 53.

53) 100 *CD* (1954), D378, D383-4, D390, D395, D401, D405-6, D411, D425-6; U.S., Congress, *Congressional Record*, 83rd Congress, 2nd Session, Volume 100, Part 6, 1954, 7424-7425; U.S., Congress, House of Representatives, Committee on Ways and Means, *Social Security Amendments of 1954*, House Report 1698, 83rd Congress, 2nd Session, 1954, 1-3, 22-25, 72-75. (Congressional Record hereinafter referred to as *CR*)

54) 100 *CR* (1954), 7418, 7426-7430.

55) 100 *CR* (1954), 7418-7419.

56) 100 *CD* (1954), D728; 100 *CR* (1954), 7364, 7418-7468.

57) 100 *CD* (1954), D519, D524, D556; U.S., Congress, Senate, Committee on Finance, *Social Security Act Amendments of 1954: Hearings on H.R. 9366*, 83rd Congress, 2nd Session, 1954, 68-77, 238-247, 421-425.

58) Hagerty, 89-90.

59) Donovan, 228-9, 275; *Time Magazine*, July 26, 1954, 10-11.

60) Hagerty, 92.

61) Hagerty, 94.

62) Hagerty, 89.

63) *Time Magazine*, July 26, 1954, 11.

64) Hagerty, 94; *Time Magazine*, July 26, 1954, 10-11; Reichard, 134-5.

65) 100 *CD* (1954), D647, D705, D709; 100 *CR* (1954), 14381, 14397, 14446; U.S., Congress, Senate, Committee on Finance, *Social Security Amendments of 1954*, Senate Report 1987, 83rd Congress, 2nd Session, 1954, 3710-3712, 3729-3732, 3782-3785, 3816.

66) House Report 1698, 23-24.

67) 100 *CD* (1954), D719, D722, D726, D729.

68) *Pub Potus, 1954*, 676.

69) *Pub Potus, 1954*, 801; *New York Times*, September 1, 1954, 1, 23; and September 2, 1954, 1, 9; Reichard, 146-7.

70) *New York Times*, September 2, 1954.

71) *U.S. News and World Report*, September 03, 1954, 44-51.

72) Ambrose, 158; *U.S. News and World Report*, December 10, 1954, 83-84.

73) Eisenhower to Earl Schaefer, 3 Feb 1954, at www.ba.ssa.gov/history/ikeletter.html.

CHAPTER THREE

Paul Douglas and the Revenge of Walter George

As the 1954 congressional elections approached, Eisenhower became more and more convinced that the future of the Republican Party depended upon its members embracing the more moderate domestic policy he envisioned. He instructed the White House Staff to start paying more attention to what he wanted and less to the desires of the legislators. As he told James Hagerty,

> The only right approach to take on all these domestic problems is a liberal approach. This party of ours and our program will not appeal to the American people unless the American people believe that we have a truly liberal program. Our hidebound reactionaries won't get to first base.[1]

The 1954 congressional elections resulted in moderate losses for the Republicans. The Democrats gained control by 1 seat in the Senate and 29 in the House. The poor showing of the Republicans at the polls, although fairly typical for an off-year election, infuriated Eisenhower, who was fed up with the Old Guard's resistance to his leadership. In a rage, he threatened to campaign across the country against them and worried little about the possibility of them forming a third party. He was determined that the Republican Party embrace his brand of progressivism.[2]

At a White House dinner on December 20, 1954, Eisenhower outlined his plan to eliminate the conservative challenge to his party leadership. The effort to consolidate the Eisenhower Republicans would begin at the national, state and local levels. The emphasis would be recruiting energetic young people to force out older politicians who had fallen behind the times. As Eisenhower explained,

> Let me remind you that if everything goes well, I will vote in only two or three or four more presidential elections but a young man or woman of 21 who believes in our party and joins it is going to be able to vote in 15 or 20 more elections. So let's go to work and build this thing up.[3]

The President hoped to sweep a new generation of Republican legislators into office with him in the 1956 elections.[4]

In the meantime, however, Eisenhower had to deal with the current composition of the 84th Congress. He focused on building a bipartisan consensus by reminding the nation at every opportunity that he had delivered on his promise of enacting improvements in social programs, most importantly Social Security. Republican campaign literature in 1954 used the creation of HEW as proof of the Republican commitment to the "well being of every individual American."[5] In his State of the Union Address on January 6, 1955, Eisenhower reiterated his concern for human problems and reasserted his belief that everyone had the right to opportunity and prosperity and that the Federal government should play an active role in securing these rights. The President also reiterated his commitment to expanding coverage under the OASI program, so long as it remained prudent to do so. He mirrored these comments in his annual budget message on January 17, 1955, emphasizing that the extension of old age and survivors insurance to 10 million more persons and the increased contribution and benefit rates enacted last year are keeping with our tradition of self reliance and will diminish dependence on charity.[6]

At the start of the 84th Congress, Eisenhower held high hopes for his social agenda. The controversy over the Bricker Amendment had abated, for the moment, and the worst of the McCarthy witch-hunts were over. The acrimony over Bricker and McCarthy had consumed so much of the nation's time and energy during the 83rd Congress that it had forced the White House into a siege mentality. Eisenhower believed that too many of his political resources had been diverted to these two issues alone and that social programs, such as national health insurance, had paid the price. Eisenhower was now free to act on the rest of his social legislative agenda, what he called the middle of the road, and he was looking forward to working with the new Democratic majorities in both houses of Congress. A moderate Republican and conservative southern Democratic coalition gave Eisenhower what amounted to a working majority in Congress. With the death of Taft and the decline of Bricker and McCarthy, the President was now, by default, the major proponent of Republican ideals. Eisenhower believed that the chances for cooperation far outweighed the possibilities of stalemate.[7]

With his own party still divided, Eisenhower forged a relationship out of necessity with the new Senate Majority Leader, Lyndon Johnson of Texas, and the new Speaker of the House, Sam Rayburn, also of Texas, both of whom had reputations as pragmatic politicians. But this required some effort on the President's part. Eisenhower's perpetual dependence on Rayburn as a safety net throughout the 1953 legislative session had grated on the Congressman. By December 1953, Rayburn was so disenchanted with Eisenhower that he often complained that while Eisenhower was a good man, he was an incompetent president. Rayburn often derisively equated Eisenhower with President Grant. He also had little respect for Eisenhower's cabinet and advisors. He considered them "very poor, mean pipsqueak(s)...the most inept and blundering administration I have ever served with."[8] However, by the end of 1954, Eisenhower was more experienced, and the influence of the Old Guard had waned due to attrition at the polls and the Republicans' status as the minority party. Eisenhower was even more dependent upon the backing of Rayburn, Johnson and the Democrats, who were now the majority party in Congress. Eisenhower saw the Democratic leadership as consensus politicians and realists. He was confident they could work together and be successful.[9]

Eisenhower worked well with Johnson and Rayburn under the mantle of bipartisanship to satisfy national interests. Rayburn set aside his personal feelings for the Eisenhower administration in deference to his responsibility to the nation as a whole. At Rayburn's insistence, the Democrats did not recklessly press their advantage against the Republicans after the 1954 elections. Rayburn wisely counseled that the preferable course of action was to remain conciliatory so that the President would not assume a bunker mentality for the upcoming legislative session. It would be far more productive to work with the progressive Republican President rather than to alienate him. In keeping with this strategy, Rayburn and Johnson were receptive to Eisenhower's overtures, as the legislative program he supported was palatable to their own interests. The President had accepted most of the New and Fair Deal economic structures, as did Johnson and Rayburn, and would continue to do so as long as they operated in a fiscally responsible manner.[10]

Meanwhile, the AMA was rapidly losing its favorable public image. So that established institutions would not lose revenue and prestige, the AMA had blocked bills to build new medical colleges. The lack of new colleges would ensure that there would be a shortage of doctors, which would allow for higher fees for services. The AMA had also opposed bills to provide a minimum of health insurance coverage for hospital and nursing home care. These bills were popular with the public and the AMA's opposition increasingly cast the doctor's organization in the image of a ruthless trade association jealously guarding the perks enjoyed by its members, rather than as a representative organization of beloved family physicians. This was amply demonstrated when the AMA inserted itself into the dispute between Congress and the President over the Bricker Amendment. Some legislators, by constitutional amendment, tried to limit the President's authority to conduct foreign relations and to limit the effects of treaties and executive agreements within the United States. The AMA supported the Bricker Amendment as part of its overall policy of opposing socialized medicine because it feared that treaties could be used as a vehicle to institute socialized medicine in America. Even against the backdrop of the Cold War, this was too paranoid for the general public to accept. The AMA's negative image became irrevocable after a half-hearted attempt to expand voluntary welfare services and charitable organizations with only preventative techniques as its goal. The AMA's message was clear: health care was the responsibility of state welfare programs, not the medical community. A reaction against the AMA set in as the American public did not like to see its doctors openly opposing measures meant to alleviate the suffering of the sick and disabled.[11]

In early 1955, liberal legislators led by Senator Paul Douglas (D-IL) and Congressman Daniel Cooper (R-NY), sought to exploit the waning influence of the AMA and expand the Social Security disability program. PL 83-761 was a start, but it was not enough. Douglas and Cooper hoped to provide monetary compensation for those suffering from serious and irremediable disabilities. In the same way that OASI was partial compensation for lost wages due to retirement or death, the Disability Insurance (DI) program would do the same for the sick and injured. Douglas realized the need for such a program because of the large number of seriously crippled men and women that he met over the years on his campaign trips through Illinois. He was able to empathize with these people because of the physical disabilities he had incurred himself as a result of his service in the Second World War. In an effort to counterbalance the influence of the AMA, Douglas obtained the backing of the American Federation of Labor, which had long been trying to get such catastrophic protection for its members. Union leaders had been angered by what they considered Eisenhower's conservative views on social insurance and the disabled. They wanted more pro-labor legislation and did not consider PL 83-761 to be nearly enough. Douglas felt his proposal was moderate and met a real and obvious need. It cut across class lines and offered support to both urban and rural interests. His strategy was to appeal to Christian compassion and to avoid the rhetoric of class struggle. Conservative Democrats actively opposed his efforts and little progress was evident through the first half of 1955.[12]

Eisenhower believed the AMA had been weakened and the President now revisited the issue of national health insurance. His efforts were hampered in the first half of 1955 by his own health problems, especially persistent cardiovascular problems that limited his vitality. While Hobby was responsible for the details, ultimately nothing could proceed without Eisenhower's authorization. Publicly, the President appeared as the picture of health, but there were indications that there was cause for worry. Eisenhower's cardiologist, Dr. Thomas Mattingly, was the chief of cardiology at Walter Reed Hospital and was scheduled at the end of 1954 to begin an assignment overseas. The White House canceled the transfer and assigned him instead to quarters on the grounds of Walter Reed Hospital so that he could be available to the President at all hours. It was apparent to Mattingly that problems were expected, considering Eisenhower's past medical history and his current lifestyle. In the meantime, action on a new national health insurance plan was put on the backburner.[13]

By June of 1955, with the White House distracted, the conservative forces opposing Douglas and Cooper on Social Security reform in Congress had them stymied until they unexpectedly received help from Georgia Democratic Senator Walter George (D-GA). George was an unlikely but welcome ally and the irony was not lost on Douglas and Cooper that George was the leader of the southern conservatives, the group blocking all social insurance reforms.[14]

Walter George was born in 1878, the son of a tenant farmer, and had grown up in poverty and deprivation in rural Georgia. He was a man of great ability and became a widely respected lawyer. He cultivated an extensive legal practice and earned acceptance from the agricultural and moneyed establishment as a safe defender of their interests. They secured his appointment to the Senate in 1922 and he rewarded them with faithful service for the next three decades.[15]

Through the Depression years, George maintained a favorable public image with his poorer constituents by creating the façade that he was an ardent New Dealer. In a speech he gave to an audience made up of impoverished Georgia farmers at the Georgia Tobacco Festival in Adel on July 1, 1936, he called President Roosevelt the greatest proponent of southern agricultural interests since Reconstruction. In reality, George opposed many New Deal programs from the beginning. He opposed Roosevelt's Court packing plan and other measures that were essential to the New Deal. In 1938, Roosevelt wanted to purge Congress of the conservative Democratic element that was opposing his efforts. Roosevelt decided to campaign against George as a warning to the growing conservative southern bloc. Roosevelt attempted to enlist Georgia's other senator, Richard Russell, in this effort, but Russell declined to participate in any purge of southern legislators. Other prominent Democrats, such as Vice President John Nance Garner of Texas, told Roosevelt not to interfere in state primary elections or he would alienate southern support for the New Deal. Roosevelt rejected this advice and continued his efforts to excommunicate George and other "Copperheads" from the Democratic Party. George and Roosevelt's other southern opponents ultimately won reelection despite his efforts against them, and Roosevelt suffered the predicted consequences.[16]

In his long Senate career, George made no real effort to help the poor or the disinherited. Instead, his political allies were big business and the propertied class, particularly the Coca-Cola Company and the Georgia Power Company. Now, in the twilight of his life, after a third of a century of faithful service, George was being pushed out by former Georgia Governor Herman Talmadge, the son of Gene Talmadge, idol of the so-called "red necks." George's supporters were deserting him and going over to the younger Talmadge. It was taken for granted that Talmadge would defeat George at the next election. George felt betrayed. With his political career nearly over, he decided to break with precedent and do something for the class he had neglected for so long—not out of some sense of regret, but for revenge. This was foreshadowed in George's remarks concerning Social Security as reported in *U.S. News and World Report* on January 2, 1953. His comments focused on the taxation issues of the OASI program and his overall tone was conservative. But he used his concern over the fiscal state of the program to hint that additional changes were on the horizon.

> *Qtn:* Do you hear of any plan for re-examination of the whole Social Security program?
>
> *Ans:* No. I think there may be some new Social Security legislation, but I don't believe it will result in the re-examination of the whole program, unless the general program should be modified into a more pay-as-you-go program....I think as the Congress approaches that problem they will see how difficult it is and probably won't undertake it within the next two years.[17]

George stated twice in the interview that changes in the system were two years away, indicating that Democratic majorities needed to be returned to Congress before these changes could occur. Now, in 1955, he was proven correct.[18]

George had made his feelings about Social Security known after the debates over H.R. 9366 in August of 1954. He didn't like the OASI provisions of the bill because he believed that Social Security was meant to benefit the working class, not white-collar professionals. The white-collar professional could finance his own retirement by investing, continuing to work at less physically demanding jobs or by selling a significant asset, such as a business, farm or practice. George did not like Social Security's increasingly compulsory nature either. He called it "creeping socialism."[19] The only part of the bill he did not object to was the disability provisions.[20]

George was a commanding figure in the Senate in 1955. At age 77, his influence was at its peak. He was the longtime Chairman of the Senate Finance Committee, until he relinquished the post to the Republicans at the start of the 83rd Congress. At the start of the 84th Congress, he became the chairman of the Senate Committee on Foreign Relations at the Eisenhower administration's request, and he supported the President's efforts over Formosa in 1955. This even earned him a kiss on the cheek from the First Lady. Backing Social Security reform did not strike George as a betrayal of the President; he had openly opposed Eisenhower before, most specifically over the Bricker Amendment in 1954. Douglas was not averse to forging an alliance with George as the two had worked together in the past, most recently in February 1954 in support of a bill to increase income tax exemptions. Douglas was interested in heading off a possible depression while George was interested in fattening the wallets of his constituents. On Social Security, Douglas wanted to help the poor and disabled while George was on a personal vendetta. As is so often the case in politics, the enemy of my enemy is my friend, and George agreed to throw his considerable support behind Douglas and Cooper, but only if his conditions were met. As Douglas later explained in his memoirs,

> It was a natural for George to make his switch, and go out as a humanitarian, rather than as a crusty conservative. But he wanted further safeguards in the bill. Men under fifty were not to receive benefits, and the funds for the new disability section of the social security law were to be isolated, so that it would not invade the reserves set up for survivors and dependents.[21]

Douglas accepted George's conditions and as promised, George delivered the southern conservatives.[22]

With George now sponsoring the proposal, it moved rapidly through Congress. The southern conservatives deplored George's sudden change in political orientation, but they could not deny him what he wanted in this circumstance. The Republican leadership had received so many favors from him in the past that it was out of the question to oppose him now. Eisenhower's reliance on the Democrats through 1953 and 1954 finally came back to haunt him. With George in the foreground, Cooper introduced the bill during an executive session of the House Committee on Ways and Means on June 21, 1955. The bill was designated H.R. 7225, and in addition to proposing a DI program for covered wage earners, the bill contained provisions for payments to disabled adult children (DAC) over the age of 18 who were disabled before the age of 22, and lowering the retirement age from 65 to 62 for women.[23]

The debate over the bill continued in committee through July 6, 1955. The committee met only in executive session and did not request any oral testimony from experts or outside sources, but it did accept written statements. In a letter to the committee dated June 21, 1955, Secretary Hobby offered her support, and the President's, for the expansion of coverage under OASI. However, she objected to the disability provisions, asserting that "Self-sufficiency and independence through rehabilitation are more important goals for the individual than dependence on cash payments."[24] She attacked the proposed cash disability program as actuarially unsound and warned that employers would use the program to unfairly discriminate against those over the age of 50.[25]

J Duffy Hancock, M.D., Chairman of the Medical Advisory Committee for SSA, outlined his objections to the disability provisions in a letter dated July 3, 1955. He believed that "total disability" was impossible to define because no standard could possibly apply to every single circumstance and that SSA could not handle the additional work.[26]

In spite of the reservations of the administration and SSA, the Ways and Means Committee approved H.R. 7225 on July 6 with the following provisions: DAC benefits payable to children age 18 and over; reduction of the retirement age for women to 62; DI benefits payable to workers age 50 and over; coverage extended to optometrists, dentists, lawyers, veterinarians, chiropractors and other professional groups; and the creation of a separate trust fund to disburse DI payments. The committee reasoned that many disabled workers did not survive to age 65 to collect their pensions, a factor which made "freeze" eligibility irrelevant in most instances. Only five percent of disabled individuals were found to be injured on the job and therefore eligible for Workmen's Compensation, so the vast majority of working Americans had no protection in the event of total disability. The cost and limited coverage offered by private plans made them prohibitive or impractical. As the committee concluded in its report,

> For the average worker, such insurance protection against income loss due to disability is not, as a practical matter, available. Your committee believes that protection under the old age and survivors insurance program should be provided in this area.[27]

The committee did not feel that the vocational rehabilitation principle would be undermined, as only those who could not be retrained would be eligible to receive cash payments.[28]

H.R. 7225 was reported to the House of Representatives for consideration on July 12, 1955. As with H.R. 9366, the debate again centered on the extension of coverage to professional classes. There was no dissent concerning the disability provisions of the bill. Representative Cooper asserted that the lack of a cash disability program was Social Security's major shortcoming and that this bill would easily rectify this omission in a fiscally sound manner. On July 18, 1955, the House passed the bill as recommended by the Ways and Means Committee by a vote of 372 to 31. None of the dissenters spoke during the debate or entered remarks in the formal record. The bill was then referred to the Senate Finance Committee.[29]

On July 26, 1955, Secretary Hobby testified before an open session of the Senate Finance Committee regarding H.R. 7225. She recommended that the committee undertake a thorough and deliberate consideration of the broad issues raised by this bill. She emphasized that HEW and the President did not support the DAC and DI portions of the bill. But this was no longer Hobby's concern; she had resigned as Secretary of HEW on July 13. HEW had been under severe criticism since April for the way it had handled the distribution of the polio vaccine. Hobby resigned her cabinet post to care for her sick husband and also because she had simply had enough. Marion Folsom was sworn in as the new Secretary of HEW on August 1, 1955. The congressional session ended on August 2 and the committee did not resume its hearings until the new session commenced in January 1956.[30]

On September 23, 1955, President Eisenhower suffered a severe heart attack that was the culmination of many months of illness. It was announced that the President had suffered a heart attack without any complications, but the information that an aneurysm existed in his heart was suppressed. Press Secretary James Hagerty controlled the dissemination of medical information to the press. News of the President's rate of recovery was exaggerated; he did not resume sitting in chairs until October 6, did not stand until October 23 and did not walk until October 29. Upon discharge from the hospital on November 11, he went to his farm in Gettysburg to convalesce. He felt bored and useless, brooding passively for extended periods of time. He returned to the Oval Office on December 23 with renewed enthusiasm, but under doctor's orders, his workday was reduced and he took frequent breaks. His overall performance was sub par and Sherman Adams confided to other members of the White House staff that "this man is not what he was."[31]

Eisenhower had organized his administration to be a team effort rather than a one-man show. Unlike the Roosevelt and Truman administrations, which had been marked by dissension and bickering among cabinet members, Eisenhower believed in delegating authority to competent subordinates. He restored the cabinet, which had declined in influence under Roosevelt and Truman, as the principal advisory body. Eisenhower believed that decentralization was the key to efficient government. As he later stated in his memoirs, "The marks of a good executive are courage in delegating work to subordinates and his own skill in coordinating and directing their effort."[32]

Unlike previous presidents, Eisenhower committed himself to frequent cabinet meetings. He devised a formal apparatus to shape cabinet agendas and then implement the decisions he made during or after the meetings. There was no voting on the issues. Eisenhower listened to the debate, without dominating the proceedings, and then made up his own mind on how to proceed. In this sense, the cabinet was a sounding board or advisory body. Eisenhower had already decided upon many of the issues that were addressed at the cabinet meetings, so the cabinet as a whole was not influential in the formation of policy. Rather, it coordinated policies that had already been decided upon. Differences of opinion on the issues were seldom expressed at cabinet meetings, although they were expressed in other forms.[33]

Eisenhower had a long-standing practice of widely seeking advice and using consultation as a method of co-opting the support of those he consulted, even if he did not take their advice. The prestige of being consulted on a matter of national concern by the President encouraged people, especially those eager to make a name for themselves, to think of themselves as part of a team, rather than a group of individuals. It was enough that the President respected their opinions to the point of consultation, but it was understood that for the good of the team, one should fall in line with the rest even if a particular recommendation was not accepted. Cabinet members were made to feel that they were general statesmen rather than jealous defenders of their departments. As a result, the administration suffered few leaks, internal feuds or public breaks with its policies. The Eisenhower administration carried out the government's business with a sense of righteousness, a result of Eisenhower's unique ability to lead people without pushing them.[34]

Theoretically, the Eisenhower administration should have been able to operate without the omnipresence of the President. On September 30, 1955, Vice President Nixon chaired a cabinet meeting in which he urged cabinet members to continue the business of the government. Work on new policies should be postponed, however, with the exception of items concerning national security. Sherman Adams and the President's doctors would decide what could be brought to Eisenhower's attention. As Social Security was not a matter of national security, the new Secretary of HEW, Marion Folsom, understood that he would maintain the Administration's opposition to H.R. 7225, but that he could not act independently. He still needed the approval of his colleagues in the cabinet. Nixon did not exude enough confidence to run the cabinet meetings efficiently and the team spirit occasionally frayed. The absence of Eisenhower's authoritative voice resulted in contentious negotiations and considerable delays to enact even stop-gap measures. It was fortunate that Eisenhower fell ill while Congress was not in session and that he sufficiently recovered before it returned. No progress on H.R. 7225 was made in the interim.[35]

On January 25, 1956, the Senate Committee on Finance met in open session to hear the testimony of Robert Meyers, Chief Actuary of SSA, on the actuarial costs of H.R. 7225. Meyers cautioned that it was difficult to predict how many disability applicants there would be under the new program, but he believed that Social Security could meet the needs of this segment of the population. Through a 1 percent increase in the FICA tax rate coupled with an expansion of covered occupations. He advocated the creation of a separate DI trust fund to safeguard the funds already earmarked for the OASI program.[36]

In subsequent days, the Finance Committee heard the testimony of Matt Triggs of the American Farm Bureau Federation, Marion Williamson of the Employment Security Agency and various representatives of advocacy groups for the blind in support of the disability provisions of the bill. On February 16, Mary Switzer of the HEW Office of Vocational Rehabilitation and E.B. Whitten of the National Rehabilitation Association both endorsed the disability provisions of the bill so long as vocational rehabilitation remained a factor of entitlement. On February 21, A.D. Marshall of the U.S. Chamber of Commerce echoed the sentiments of Switzer and Whitten. Testifying against the disability provisions of the bill were a large number of doctors representing the AMA and the American Academy of General Practitioners. Dr. Cyrus W Anderson spoke for many of his medical colleagues when he warned that

> The cash disability provision would work an unfair hardship on the medical profession....The doctor's assignment is to cure and comfort people who are sick. It's an even more difficult responsibility to make decisions which directly relate to the patient's income....There will be doctors who aren't above certifying a dubious disability. There will be others who will lose patients because they will refuse to cooperate with a malingerer. No matter how carefully you plan ways to avoid abuses, they will continue to exist and could easily become rampant.[37]

The private insurance lobby opposed the bill as well. Representatives of the insurance companies testified that cash disability benefits would encourage sloth and serve as a disincentive to overcome a physical problem. They were also concerned that a federal disability program would discourage people from purchasing private disability insurance.[38]

On March 1, 1956, the Senate Finance Committee heard the testimony of Henry Viscardi, the President of Abilities, Inc., a company based in southern New York. Viscardi, had been born without legs and owned and operated a successful company that employed only those who would be considered permanently disabled and unable to work under the guidelines of H.R. 7225. He described the many positive experiences he had had in running his company and emphasized that his employees preferred to work rather than be on the public dole. Viscardi believed that vocational rehabilitation worked and that providing sheltered work environments was a viable enterprise which would be undermined by the disability provisions of H.R. 7225.[39]

The President still considered disability benefit programs to be a function of state and local government, but he did not want to get caught up in the backlash against the AMA by publicly opposing any kind of disability program, federal or state. To decry the efforts going on in Congress to create a disability program under Social Security would seem to run counter to his rhetoric that the situation of the poor and downtrodden must be addressed. The distinctions of federalism meant nothing to most people, no matter how well argued. Eisenhower could not even use his own recent health problems as an example. On the surface, he appeared to be his own best argument for the effectiveness of the 1954 amendments; he had suffered a severe ill-ness, was out of work for a time, recovered, and went back to work. Realistically, he did not have to file an application with Social Security. He did not have to go through a course of vocational rehabilitation. He did not have to wait months or up to a year for a determination on his status. No matter how long he was unable to perform, his job was still waiting for him when he returned and he suffered no loss in pay. Most important of all, he had access to the best medical care in the country, possibly the world, at no cost. If he came out publicly against the pro-posed DI program, he would appear to be a hypocrite at best.

Eisenhower still advocated a national reinsurance health program and opposed the expansion of Social Security entitlements. He addressed both of these issues in a carefully worded message to Congress on the Nation's Health Program on January 26, 1956, the day after hearings began in the Senate Finance Committee on H.R. 7225. The President agreed that further action was needed to improve the level of health care available to the people, and he called for a partnership between "private and governmental enterprise" to advance the national welfare.[40] Eisenhower specifically asked Congress for 250 million dollars to build more medical teaching and research facilities, but he also called for a "pooling" arrangement between the government and private insurers. "Pooling" would provide health insurance coverage to individuals who suffered from catastrophic illness, a severe handicap or poor health due to advanced age. It would also assist those who lived in impoverished, rural areas. Eisenhower concluded by reiterating that the role of the federal government was to support private, state and local efforts to foster the greater good without compromising the basic freedoms of all Americans. His message to legislators was clear; he never mentioned the DI program in H.R. 7225, calling instead for increased funds for the vocational rehabilitation program. The President's "pooling" proposal for national health insurance was simply brushed aside and never even considered by Congress.[41]

HEW Secretary Folsom testified before the Senate Finance Committee on March 22, 1956 to accentuate the Administration's opposition to H.R. 7225. Folsom stated his own position on the bill as well as the President's. The administration believed that Social Security was not the best way to aid the severely disabled worker. The administration was opposed in general to any expansion of entitlements under Social Security and urged instead that other social welfare programs at the state and local levels be enhanced. The DI program would require the creation of a separate trust fund from OASI and a corresponding FICA tax increase, which Eisenhower emphatically opposed because of his general reluctance to raise taxes or expand the size of the federal government. Folsom asserted that

> In the light of recent tax increases and the scheduled increase in 1960, an additional major tax increase should not be imposed now on the 70 million workers covered by the OASI system....For the reasons I have already stated, the provisions of H.R. 7225 to....provide cash disability benefits under OASI should not be adopted.[42]

Folsom was questioned harshly by the committee members, who did not readily accept his rationale for opposing a cash disability program. He was attacked primarily on the improbability of being able to rehabilitate disabled workers over the age of 50.[43]

The Senate Finance Committee delayed its executive sessions on H.R. 7225 so that the House Ways and Means Committee could hear additional testimony. Favorable testimony was heard from April 12, 1956, through April 23, 1956, from SSA Commissioner Charles Schottland, Doctor Martha Eliot of SSA's Children's Bureau and Doctor Jacobus Tenbroek of the National Federation for the Blind, among others.[44]

On April 24, 1956, the Senate Finance Committee met in executive sessions to consider H.R. 7225. The bill approved by the Committee contained provisions for widows to receive survivor benefits at age 62; payment of cash benefits for DAC's; and the extension of coverage to additional types of agricultural workers and ministers working out-side the United States. The Committee struck from the bill the sections providing for payment of cash benefits to disabled workers and the corresponding tax increase that would have accompanied it. The Committee rejected the DI provisions after considering the difficulty in making disability determinations, the availability of assistance under state and local programs, the significant strides made in voca-tional rehabilitation, the uncertainty as to the future costs of a cash dis-ability program and the need to study and evaluate other existing disability programs. Senators George and Douglas remained uncon-vinced and undaunted. They prepared to argue for the DI program on the floor of the Senate.[45]

To the surprise of no one, on May 9, 1956, George held a press con-ference and announced his retirement from the Senate effective with the close of the current session, in July. He cited old age and poor health as his reasons, but it was common knowledge that the polls showed that Talmadge would defeat him in the September primary. Eisenhower publicly stated that George's expertise as Chairman of the Senate Committee on Foreign Relations would be sorely missed. So that the Administration could continue to make use of his counsel, the

President created a new post, U.S. Ambassador to NATO, and offered it to George, who graciously accepted.[46]

Eisenhower did not have to offer George, a Democrat, a new position within the administration. After all, he would be out of office in July. But even in retirement, George could still carry considerable influence as a liaison to the Senate, especially in foreign policy. Eisenhower seized the opportunity to co-opt a dissident voice and demonstrate that he was above partisan politics in the wake of the bitter June 1956 struggle between Congress and the President over foreign aid appropriations. The position was also a reward to George for supporting the foreign policy of the President against the wishes of the conservative constituents in his home state. To a lesser degree, Eisenhower was also hoping that this gesture would lead George to reconsider his position on H.R. 7225. It did not.[47]

On May 14, 1956, the President addressed the Conference on Occupational Safety and make known his feelings on H.R. 7225. Eisenhower made it very clear that it was the responsibility of the business community to see to the safety of its workers in order to lessen the need for disability programs. He warned against using disability as an excuse to let the federal government extend its authority into the workplace, and he urged state and local governments to exercise more vigilance to prevent this from happening. The President concluded:

> I don't know how many of the individuals in this audience have ever had the task—almost the daily task—of writing letters of condolence to families that have lost a dear one....[W]hen you stop to think of fourteen thousand bereaved families in this country every year, occasioned by preventable accidents, it is indeed—to such a person as myself—a tragic fact....So I believe that such people as yourselves have the solution largely in your hands. The Federal Government can do little. The President can call a conference to bring you together so that you may exchange ideas; so that

each of you may gain some inspiration from the fact that so many do come to look into this thing and show their determination to do something about it.[48]

The Senate began deliberations on H.R. 7225 on July 13, 1956. Various amendments were attached to the bill, including the George amendment which provided for cash disability benefits at age 50 for disabled workers. The Senate devoted the bulk of it time to debating the Long amendment, which concerned formulas for federal matching contributions to state welfare programs. Senate Majority Leader Lyndon Johnson favored the George amendment and was keenly aware of the substantial Republican opposition to it. He used his influence to limit the debate on the amendment to three hours in order to discourage open-ended criticism.[49]

Speaking in favor of the George amendment were Senators Henry Jackson (D-WA), Herbert Lehman (D-NY) and George himself. Jackson called the DI program "humane"[50] and stated that he could not fathom the President's objection to it. He did not believe that Secretary Folsom's testimony to the Senate Finance Committee truly reflected the opinion of everyone at HEW, and he charged that the tactic of delaying implementation of the DI program for further study was simply "a rear-guard action against social progress."[51] George made an eloquent speech describing the medical and financial hardships faced by some 400,000 disabled Americans, trying to shame the Senate into approving the DI program.[52] George stated it was

singularly distressing and very strange in the year 1956 to hear the arguments of those who say we can rely upon Public Assistance to meet the needs of those who are disabled. We have not followed this principle with respect to the aged, widows, dependent children or the unemployed….As a progressive, enlightened nation we have adopted the policy that assistance is the second line of defense…we must now apply the contributory social insurance principle to the risk of permanent total disability.[53]

Senators Harry Byrd (D-VA) and Carl Curtis (R-NE) led the opposition to the George amendment. Byrd argued that Social Security could not afford to finance the DI program proposed in the bill and that it was too complex for SSA to administer, even with the aid of the states. He also read a letter written by Doctor Elmer Hess, the President of the AMA. Hess opposed the DI provisions of H.R. 7225, asserting that the vocational rehabilitation program enacted in 1954 was a success and what was proposed now was fiscally unsound. He warned that being on the federal dole would be crippling to the psyche of the disabled. The DI program, in his opinion, was an insult to disabled workers that was tantamount to the government bribing them to stay out of the workforce. It told them that their efforts to return to work were not wanted and it provided an institutionalized reason to avoid vocational rehabilitation. Byrd then reiterated the success of Henry Viscardi's company, Abilities, Inc., as evidence showing the benefits of vocational rehabilitation. As the Chairman of the Finance Committee, Byrd defended his committee's decision to reject the disability provisions of the bill. Curtis supplemented Byrd's remarks, asserting that DI provisions were a noble idea but, if enacted, would be perverted into something unconscionable that could not yet be foreseen. He also warned that the decision-making process was arbitrary and that inequities would be inevitable.[54]

The highlight of the debate over the George amendment was an exchange between Senators Russell Long (D-LA) and Wallace Bennett (R-UT). Bennett echoed the sentiments of Senator Byrd and favored vocational rehabilitation over cash benefits. He believed that the states could handle the burden of caring for those who were so severely disabled that they could never return to work. Long then informed the Senate that the largest single cause of disability in America was hardening of the arteries and he asked Bennett directly what benefit a cardiac patient would derive from a course of vocational rehabilitation.

Bennett responded by discussing the case of his own brother, who had suffered three heart attacks and was still working as a supermarket manager. Bennett was quick to add that just like the President, his brother had readjusted his lifestyle and resumed his daily regimen. Long countered by pointing out the significant difference between the job responsibilities of a sedentary manager and the physically laboring subordinate. Long had made Bennett's point for him. Bennett noted that it was expected that the manager would return to his old job, while the common worker would undergo a course of vocational rehabilitation to learn a job that was not as physically taxing.[55]

In the end, the George amendment passed 47 to 45 in almost a strict party line vote. H.R. 7225 as a whole then passed the Senate 90-0. Senators Byrd, George, Robert Kerr (D-OK), Allen Frear (D-DE), Eugene Millikin (R-CO), Edward Martin (R-PA) and John Williams (R-DE) were then appointed to a conference committee to negotiate with their counterparts from the House.[56]

From July 20 to July 26, 1956, the Conference Committee on Social Security met in executive sessions to consider H.R. 7225. The legislators finally agreed that more categories of workers should be covered under Social Security; that DI and DAC programs should be created; and that these new benefits should be paid out of a separate trust fund, called the DI trust fund. All of this would be financed by a .25% increase in the FICA tax rate. The separate trust fund was in response to fears that disability payments might bleed the OASI fund and disrupt the actuarial soundness of the OASI program. In order to prevent such an occurrence, strict eligibility requirements were also mandated. To meet the medical requirement alone, an individual needed to be suffering from a terminal illness or a crippling impairment. Any disabled person who demonstrated the residual capacity to perform any kind of sedentary job would be deemed ineligible for benefits. The greater the range of education, the greater the chance of denial as, theoretically, there would be a broader scope of sedentary jobs that the disabled person could perform. Prejudice against hiring the disabled or the job market in the disabled person's locality was not taken into consideration. If an individual could theoretically perform a job that was listed in the national economy, benefits would be denied. In the event that the DI program was not successful, the separate trust fund would ensure that it could not endanger the payment of retirement or survivor benefits. On July 26, 1956, the House adopted conference report 2936 and the Senate followed suit on July 27.[57]

The President had no choice but to sign H.R. 7225 into law. The bill was enormously popular and enough legislators supported it to override his veto. His feelings on the issue had not changed since January 1956, nor had his concern about the pubic response if he opposed the bill in an election year. Any objection to the bill based on the small increase in the FICA tax rate was weak. The current tax rate was only 2 percent, and because Eisenhower had brought an additional ten million workers into the OASI program in 1954, the tax increase to 4 percent could be delayed until 1975. Some consolation was taken from the fact that he had gotten additional provisions that he favored passed by Congress, such as extending coverage to more workers and an increase in funding to provide for more social workers to assist in vocational rehabilitation. In addition, SSA reassured the President that the DI program would not upset the social insurance consensus and jeopardize any future plans for national health care. H.R. 7225 became PL 84-880 on August 1, 1956, at which time the President offered these remarks:

> Congress also modified somewhat the original proposal (in order) to provide disability benefits at age 50 or above. A separate trust fund was established for the disability program in an effort to minimize the effects of the special problems in this field on the other parts of the program—retirement and survivor protection. We will, of course, endeavor to administer the disability provisions efficiently and effectively, in cooperation with the States. I also pledge increasing emphasis on efforts to help rehabilitate the disabled so that they may return to useful employment.[58]

Eisenhower still maintained that some aspects of the bill were "unwise" and that it was unfair to burden Social Security with "something I don't think should be there." But when asked to elaborate, the President refused.[59]

In the grand scheme of national events, PL 84-880 was largely ignored, as indicated by the press conference that took place after the President signed the bill into law. The only question asked about the new law was whether the administration thought that the age 50 requirement for DI entitlement should be higher. Eisenhower gave an evasive, non-committal response that demonstrated his lack of enthusiasm for the whole DI program. In contrast to his signing of the 1954 amendments, when the President gushed with enthusiasm, this time he was rather subdued. He never mentioned PL 84-880 in any future public statement, nor did he attempt to take any credit for it.[60]

Meanwhile, Walter George took great pleasure in the way he left the Senate. George was a dour individual, even in the best of moods, but he seemed to enjoy immensely being able to strike back at those supporters who had deserted him. Senator Douglas later commented in his memoirs that "George took pleasure in this during his few remaining years. Once, he even smiled when he met me—an unprecedented occurrence."[61]

The blueprint for the DI program appeared simple. The disabled applicant would go to his local Social Security office where he would be assisted in filling out forms and filing his application. The severity of the applicant's impairment and how it affected his chances for vocational rehabilitation would be determined in state run offices that were part of each state's existing vocational rehabilitation program. These offices were already experienced in gathering medical and vocational evidence and deciding whether a person met the criteria to be considered disabled. On the political level, state control of disability decisions took some of the menace out of the extension of federal authority. States could be expected to exercise more caution than the federal government in declaring someone eligible for a disability pension. On the psychological level, letting the states administer the program put a positive spin on a negative program. Rather than a program for labor force dropouts, disability insurance became a means of putting disability applicants in contact with rehabilitation counselors. Those beyond redemption would be allowed to retire. Others would be enrolled in vocational rehabilitation programs, retrained for something their illness or injury would allow them to do, and sent off in search of gainful employment. Such a turn around would revitalize the applicants desire to work, so the theory went.[62]

By the end of 1956, Eisenhower's social insurance agenda was in shambles. While he could point to numerous other successes, his goals of controlling the expansion of Social Security and enacting a program of national health insurance had eluded him. The country was prosperous. The Cold War continued, but the nation was at peace. Vital legislation had been enacted, such as the Eisenhower Interstate Highway System, hydropower development, the St Lawrence Seaway project, federal grants-in-aid to schools and hospitals and many others. But the President was still bitter. He was bitter because he had had Social Security moving in the direction he desired until Walter George took it away from him. He was bitter because he could not build a consensus for his national health insurance plans. This was demonstrated again when Congress ignored Secretary Folsom's proposal of June 29, 1956, to enact a "pooling" method of providing national health insurance. With his best years in office already behind him, Eisenhower's second term would be custodial at best in the area of social insurance.[63]

References: Chapter Three

1) Hagerty, 106.

2) Hagerty, 106, 129.

3) Hagerty, 145.

4) Hagerty, 145-6.

5) Branyan and Larsen, 410.

6) *Pub Potus, 1955*, 86-101; Branyan and Larsen, 469.

7) Branyan and Larsen, 234, 429-31.

8) Hardeman and Bacon, 379, 392-3.

9) Hardeman and Bacon, 379, 392-3; Branyan and Larsen, 429-30.

10) Ambrose, 160; Alexander, 34-5; Richardson, 45-6; Hardeman and Bacon, 379- 380, 385.

11) Douglas, 390-3; Tananbaum, 118-119; David 57-61.

12) Douglas, 391; Parmet, 326.

13) Robert Gilbert, *The Mortal Presidency: Illness and Anguish in the White House* (New York: Basic Books, 1992), 82-86.

14) Douglas, 391.

15) Douglas, 391; Tananbaum, 144.

16) Paul Boller, Jr, *Presidential Anecdotes* (New York: Viking Penguin, 1982), 294-296; Gilbert C. Fite, *Richard B Russell, Jr.: Senator From Georgia* (Chapel Hill: University of North Carolina Press, 1991), 142, 163-4; Tananbaum, 144.

17) *U.S. News and World Report*, January 2, 1953, 34-5

18) Douglas, 391.

19) 100 *CR* (1954), 15409.

20) 100 *CR* (1954), 15409.

21) Douglas, 391.

22) Donovan, 216, 341-2, 306-7; Douglas, 391; Tananbaum, 144-5; Adams, 108-9, 130-131.

23) 101 *CD* (1955), D421; Douglas, 391-2; U.S., Congress, House of Representatives, Committee on Ways and Means, *Social Security Amendments of 1955*, House Report 1189, 84th Congress, 1st Session, 1955, 1-7.

24) House Report 1189, 60.

25) 101 *CD* (1955), D430, D436, D440, D458, D479; House Report 1189, 58-62.

26) House Report 1189, 65.

27) House Report 1189, 6.

28) 101 *CD* (1955), D430, D436, D440, D458, D479; House Report 1189.

29) 101 *CD* (1955), D501, D512, D521; 101 *CR* (1955), 10254, 10768, 10798-10799.

30) 101 *CD* (1955), D564; Donovan, 322-3; Adams, 306-11.

31) Gilbert, 86-94, 118; Adams 191-2.

32) Eisenhower, 134-5; Alexander, 34-5.

33) Richardson, 35-6; Greenstein, 114-115; Parmet, 176; Adams 5-7.

34) Richardson, 35-6; Greenstein, 116; Parmet, 176.

35) Gilbert 119-126; Adams 185-6.

36) 102 *CD* (1956), D44, D48; U.S., Congress, Senate, Committee on Finance, *Social Security Act Amendments of 1955: Hearings on H.R. 7225*, 84th Congress, 2nd Session, 1956, 13-39.

37) *Hearings on H.R. 7225, 359.*

38) 102 *CD* (1956), D44, D48, D52, D55, D60, D75, D78, D84, D88, D102, D107, D110, D119, D123, *Hearings on H.R 7225*, 356-1035.

39) 102 *CD* (1956), D39, D128, D136; *Hearings on H.R 7225*, 1035-1043.

40) *Pub Potus 1956*, 196-7.

41) *New York Times*, January 27, 1956, 1, 10; *U. S. News and World Report*, August 3, 1956, 50.

42) 102 *CD* (1956), D191.

43) 102 *CD* (1956), D191; *Hearings on H.R 7225*, 1225-1280.

44) 102 *CD* (1956), D232, D239, D256, D263.

45) 102 *CD* (1956), D265, D270, D298, D302, D308, D320, D336-7, D361-2, D373, D395; U.S., Congress, Committee on Finance, *Social Security Amendments of 1956*, Senate Report 2133, 84th Congress, 2nd Session, 1956, 3-4.

46) *New York Times*, May 10, 1956, 1, 17; *U.S. News and World Report*, July 27, 1956, 20.

47) *Time Magazine*, July 9, 1956, 9-10; Adams 130-1.

48) *Pub Potus, 1956*, 490-1.

49) 102 *CD* (1956), D558; 100 *CR* (1956), 12995, 13032.

50) 102 *CR* (1956), 13023.

51) 102 *CR* (1956), 13023.

52) 102 *CR* (1956), 12995-13051.

53) 102 *CR* (1956), 13037-13038.

54) 102 *CR* (1956), 13033-13034, 13046-13047, 13051.

55) 102 *CR* (1956), 13035-13036.

56) 102 *CD* (1956), D573; 100 *CR* (1956), 13056,13567; *U.S. News and World Report*, July 27, 1956, 20; *Time Magazine*, July 30, 1956, 9.

57) 102 *CD* (1956), D602, D606, D 635, D 636, D637; U.S., Congress, House of Representatives, Committee on Ways and Means, *Social Security Amendments of 1956*, Conference Report 2936, 84th Congress, 2nd Session, 1956, 3954-3976; Bernstein, 187, 214-215.

58) *Pub Potus, 1956*, 639.

59) Berkowitz, 165; *U.S. News and World Report*, July 27, 1956, 43-45; *New York Times*, August 2, 1956, 1, 49.

60) *Pub Potus 1956*, 639-640.

61) Douglas, 391-2.

62) Berkowitz, 165-6.

63) Dwight D. Eisenhower, *The White House Years, Vol.2, Waging Peace, 1956-1961* (Garden City NY: Doubleday and Company, 1965), 17.

CHAPTER FOUR

Congress Takes Control

The remaining years of the Eisenhower Administration were marked by rather effortless expansions and refinements of the Social Security program, despite the President's efforts to the contrary. After the 1954 amendments, Eisenhower did not make any new legislative proposals concerning Social Security. A stroke suffered in November 1957 hampered Eisenhower's effectiveness as President throughout his second term. Combined with an overall loss of stamina due to his persistent cardiac condition, Eisenhower was forced into a more passive role in his attempts to keep Social Security in line with his own ideals. Control over the evolution of the OASDI programs was effectively ceded to Congress and legislators responded to the desires of a very vocal, and up to this time ignored, segment of society. With the 1954 amendments, the federal government had acknowledged some responsibility for the care of the disabled. Subsequently, a lack of coordinated and vigorous opposition to the liberalization of that definition of responsibility allowed for all of the amendments that followed. With Congress, and more specifically the Democrats, initiating the legislative proposals to aid the aged and disabled, Eisenhower and the Republicans found it difficult to resist without casting themselves as villains. In addition, the business community lacked leverage in the ongoing debate as the FICA tax rate was still minimal (2.25% in 1957) and benefit payments remained modest. Democratic support was essential to implement other legislative programs unrelated to Social Security, so Eisenhower was careful not to criticize the Democrats too harshly.[1]

Eisenhower's passive resistance to Social Security expansion began with his re-election campaign in 1956. The Republican Party platform offered minimal support to the DI program, which was barely mentioned; in contrast, the Republicans took credit for the expansion of Social Security's coverage to additional professions. The platform reiterated Eisenhower's belief that

> In all those things which deal with people, be liberal, be human. In all those things which deal with people's money, or their economy, or their form of government, be conservative.[2]

The Republicans took credit for creating the Department of HEW and promised "to seek extension and perfection of a sound social security system."[3] In contrast, the Democratic Party platform in 1956 reveled in their Social Security triumphs, primarily the 1956 amendments. The Democrats pledged

> continued support of legislation to improve employment opportunities of physically handicapped persons....By lowering the retirement age for women and for the disabled person, the Democratic 84th Congress pioneered two great advances in Social Security, over the bitter opposition of the Eisenhower Administration. We shall continue our efforts to broaden and strengthen this program by increasing benefits to keep pace with improving standards of living.[4]

Eisenhower was easily reelected, but he again faced a Congress controlled by the Democrats.[5]

In his Annual Budget Message, delivered to Congress on January 16, 1957, Eisenhower restated his opposition to additional amendments to the Social Security Act. He preferred to address social issues through budgetary actions rather than enacting new legislation, although he believed that throwing money at a problem was not necessarily the solution. As an alternative, he called upon the states to make their social welfare programs more efficient. This budgetary message began a trend which continued for the remainder of Eisenhower's presidency. When the costs of social programs he had opposed skyrocketed, he cried, "I told you so!"[6]

On March 21, 1957, Representatives Daniel Reed (R-NY) and John Sherman Cooper (R-KY) introduced a bill extending filing deadlines for disability "freeze" applications and removing the veterans' pension offset. The existing law provided for one year of retroactivity concerning disability "freeze" applications, but only if they were filed before July 1, 1957. The proposed legislation would extend the filing deadline to July 1, 1958, to protect the rights of workers who did not meet the earnings requirements to qualify for monthly cash benefits under the DI program created by the 1956 amendments. In addition, Reed and Cooper want to repeal the provision in the 1956 amendments that required the reduction, or offset, of DI payments if the beneficiary were receiving a disability benefit under another Federal program. The House Committee on Ways and Means considered the bill, designated H.R. 6191, in executive session for one day and then reported it favorably to the House. Cooper and Reed briefly addressed the House in support of the bill on March 28 and H.R. 6191 was passed by a unanimous voice vote on the same date. It was then referred to the Senate.[7]

The Senate Finance Committee considered H.R. 6191 on June 13, 1957. The committee agreed to the filing date extension, but struck from the bill the provision removing the veteran's pension offset until the financial consequences could be studied. The revised bill was reported to the full Senate on June 17, 1957, where deliberations began and concluded on July 3, 1957. Senator Jacob Javits (R-NY), with the support of Charles Potter (R-MI) and Frank Carlson (R-KS), restored the House version by rejecting the Finance Committee's report.

Senators did not want to appear biased against the disabled or veterans. The provisions were minor, but they were significant to those depending on the benefits in question. The Senate then approved H.R. 6191 by a unanimous voice vote and sent it to the President. Eisenhower signed it into law with absolutely no fanfare. The press did not cover the signing and the President did not issue a statement.[8]

In his Annual Budget Message to Congress the following year, Eisenhower hinted that all of the awful things he had predicted about Social Security expansion were coming true. He pointed out that the subsequent amendments to the existing OASDI and public assistance laws were making the programs more expensive as the federal matching shares increased with each amendment. He wanted the states to show greater fiscal responsibility so that the federal role could be reduced. Eisenhower's hopes were at cross-purposes with the 1956 amendments, however; the DI program was meant to alleviate some of the financial strains placed by the disabled on state and local welfare programs. Eisenhower indicated that the administration was studying how to maintain the trust funds and simplify employer paperwork, and would submit legislation to solve these problems in 1960. This was a warning to the states to prepare themselves both fiscally and bureaucratically to assume more of the burdens from the federal government in social welfare programs.[9]

Congress was not prepared to wait two years or longer to respond to the pressures of special interest groups who were pushing for a resolution to some of the inequities in the DI program. On June 16, 1958, Congressman Reed introduced a proposal to refine the existing program. Designated H.R. 13549, Reed's bill called for payments to the dependent spouses and children under the age of 18 of disabled wage earners, removal of workmen's compensation offset, extension of the "freeze" application deadline to July 1, 1961, and refinement of insured status requirements. Workmen's compensation offset functioned on the same principle as the now repealed veterans' pension offset: if a DI beneficiary were also entitled to any kind of payment from a state disability program, his DI benefit would be reduced. The

1954 amendments established *currently* insured status (i.e. the minimum earnings requirement) for "freeze" as earnings in at least 18 of the previous 39 months. The 1956 amendments established *fully* insured status (i.e. the minimum earnings requirement) for DI payments as earnings in at least 60 of the previous 120 months. To avoid the anomalous situation that could occur after July 1, 1961, in which a worker could qualify for "freeze" and not be eligible for any DI payments, Reed's bill proposed eliminating the *currently* insured status provision and making *fully* insured status the requirement for both the "freeze" and DI programs.[10]

Secretary of HEW Marion Folsom testified before the Ways and Means Committee on June 16, 1958. Folsom explained that the administration opposed the bill it was actuarially unsound. Any increase in benefit payments or expansion of entitlement would require a tax increase, either now or in the future. It was not good economic policy to mortgage the future to pay for the present, Folsom asserted; he emphasized that the proposal conflicted with the President's opposition to increasing taxes. Folsom argued that now was not the time for additional reforms because SSA was not yet current with the backlog in claims generated by the 1956 amendments.[11]

Nelson Cruikshank of the AFL testified in favor of H.R. 13549. Cruikshank claimed that the existing benefit programs were not comprehensive and that many workers of varying circumstance desperately needed assistance. Forcing people onto welfare raised issues of dignity and did not provide benefits equal to the current cost of living. The AFL supported any liberalization of the current Social Security laws, so long as increases in the tax rate were kept to a minimum.[12]

General hearings on the bill concluded on June 30, 1958, and the Committee on Ways and Means reported the bill to the full House on July 28, 1958, by a vote of 24 to 1. Support for the bill was widespread and bipartisan, and at the request of Representatives Reed and Wilbur Mills (D-AK), the ranking minority and majority members of the Ways and Means Committee, debate was limited to four hours, ostensibly to prevent the possible defeat of the bill through deliberate efforts to confuse the issues involved.[13]

The House of Representatives considered H.R. 13549 on July 31, 1958. Representatives Mills and Reed both argued that there was a real need to provide the families of disabled wage earners with additional income. Since Social Security Disability payments were partial compensation for wages lost due to disability, it seemed logical that dependents should also receive partial compensation for the resources that would have been allocated to them by the wage earner. Mills and Reed similarly contended that Social Security benefits should not be reduced when a recipient was also entitled to Workmen's Compensation payments. They were different programs, funded by different taxes; one was federal and one was state, and a disabled wage earner should not be penalized if he or she were an honest taxpayer. It was revealed during the debate that the bill had been crafted with the cooperation of officials in HEW, although the administration officially supported only the reforms changing the filing deadlines for "freeze" and insured status requirements. Representative Aime Forand (R-RI) also spoke in favor of the bill, asserting that it would improve the standard of living for the disadvantaged, but argued that it did not go far enough. It was pointed out that crippled children with able parents would still be left without assistance.[14]

H.R. 13549 passed the House later that day by a vote of 374-2. The two dissenters, Representatives Bruce Alger (D-TX) and Noah Mason (R-IL), did not formally address the legislature. Alger had his objections recorded in the *Congressional Record* after the vote. He believed the bill was fiscally unsound and would lead to a higher rate of inflation.[15]

The Senate Finance Committee initiated hearings on H.R. 13549 on August 8, 1958. Arthur Flemming, who had succeeded Folsom as Secretary of HEW on August 1, reiterated the administration's opposition to the bill, primarily on actuarial grounds. He reported that the trust funds were currently declining and the situation would not be corrected until the next legislated tax increase , which was scheduled to go into effect in 1965. To enact changes in the program now would have unforeseen adverse consequences, he warned. Fleming advised that the matter required additional study and urged that action on the bill be delayed at least until after January 1, 1959, when the administration was prepared to make its own report on the status of Social Security's financing.[16]

The committee conducted hearings on the bill through August 13, 1958. Various legislators and Labor Department officials testified about those portions of the bill that concerned federal bloc grants to the states for local welfare programs. Once again, the disability provisions of the bill were seldom addressed.[17]

On August 14, 1958, the committee reported H.R. 13549 to the floor and the bill was debated on August 15. Senators Hubert Humphrey (D-MN), Ralph Yarborough (D-TX), Richard Neuberger (D-OR), Knowland (R-CA) and Warren Magnuson (D-WA) all spoke in favor of the bill, asserting that it would increase the standard of living of the families of the disabled. It would also fight inflation by maintaining income levels relative to the cost of living. Senator Russell Long (D-LA) believed that the administration was using scare tactics by claiming that the bill was actuarially unsound. Senator Thomas Kuchel (R-CA) warned that the benefit increases proposed were too small to make a difference in the quality of people's lives and would increase the rate of inflation, but, in the end, even those with doubts voted for H.R. 13549, which passed the Senate 79-0.[18]

The Conference Committee on H.R. 13549 met briefly and agreed to the Senate version of the bill. The final bill passed the House and Senate on August 23, 1958, by voice votes and was cleared for the President on the same date.[19]

Eisenhower signed H.R. 13549 into law on August 29, 1958, despite its divergence from the recommendations in his Annual Budget Message. The FICA tax rate was increased from 2.25% to 2.5% and the annual taxable wage base was also increased from $4200 to $4800 to support benefit payments to the dependents of disabled wage earners. The federal matching share for welfare grants to the states was also increased. The workmen's compensation offset was abolished.

Retroactive filing deadlines for disability applications were increased to one year and insured status requirements were clarified. In signing the bill, the President tried to put a positive spin on a piece of legislation that he simply hated. He praised the OASI changes, calling them a "significant forward step" necessary to "strengthen the financial condition of this system in the years immediately ahead and over the long term future."[20] He noted that the FICA tax rate increase was needed to correct an actuarial imbalance in the trust funds. In his brief statement to the press, Eisenhower acknowledged his continuing lack of support for the DI program through selective omission. He did not mention the new DI provisions.[21]

Public reaction was mixed. Those who received Social Security Benefits supported the higher benefit amounts. Younger workers, however, grudgingly accepted the higher payroll taxes needed to shore up the system so that it would provide for them in later years. Employers, including some agricultural entities, resented the increase in their tax liability. One unfortunate example concerned the Amish in Ohio. An Amish sect living in Canton had quoted scripture to justify its refusal to pay FICA tax. In response, the federal government confiscated livestock and sold it at public auction to satisfy the outstanding tax levies. Their religious beliefs also prevented the Amish from accepting Social Security benefits and no record existed of any member of the Amish community ever receiving benefits. Religious objections, as well as fiscal and political arguments against Social Security's compulsory nature, fell upon deaf ears.[22]

On January 19, 1959, Eisenhower sent his annual Budget Message to Congress for fiscal 1960. He reiterated his opposition to the expanding federal role in state and welfare programs, and argued again that federal responsibility for income maintenance to the aged and disabled should be limited solely to the OASDI programs. The President believed that the federal government had reached the limit of the aid it could offer to social programs. Under his administration, 90% of the nation's workers were now covered under Social Security; there were now 13.7 million beneficiaries receiving over a billion dollars in payments annually. This,

Eisenhower believed, was plenty. He again reminded Congress that fed-eral expenditures for public assistance grants to the states continued to increase and given the federal monies invested in SSA, he wanted to break this cycle of dependency on the part of the states. Eisenhower called for the states to take greater responsibility for their social welfare programs.[23]

Similarly, in 1960 when Eisenhower sent his annual Budget Message to Congress for fiscal 1961, he praised the efficiency of the Social Security Administration, noting that its overhead was only two percent of all the FICA tax collected annually. He then chastised the states for their contrasting inefficiency and took them, and Congress, to task for not finding a way to decrease federal expenditures for local welfare programs.[24]

In response to the President's pleas, legislators sought to reduce the cost of welfare programs to the federal government and the states by relaxing the non-medical requirements of the DI program. Representative Reed introduced H.R. 12580 in March 1960, which focused on the age 50 cut-off for entitlement. Originally part of the 1956 amendments, this provision mandated that a worker must be at least 50 years of age in order to qualify for DI benefits. No public hear-ings were held on the bill, and after the committee considered it in executive sessions, H.R. 12580 was reported to the House on June 9, 1960. Debate commenced on June 22, and in response to a request from Representatives Mills, debate was limited to four hours. Mills explained that the finer points of the bill were too complicated to be rehashed on the floor in open debate and argued that the House should trust that the Committee on Ways and Means had fulfilled its obligations properly.[25]

The debate initially focused on the minimum age requirement, but then moved on to questions over the new Trial Work Period (TWP) provisions. The TWP allowed for workers currently receiving DI bene-fits to return to work and earn as much money as they wanted, but only for a period of nine months. The debate quickly degenerated into hostility as the legislators re-ignited the old argument over a national program of health insurance versus socialized medicine. Representative Mills pronounced the bill actuarially sound and asserted that it would alleviate the hardships of those disabled at a young age. The TWP provision would encourage vocational rehabilitation by creating a way for beneficiaries to test their ability to work without jeopardizing their entitlement to benefits. Representative Mason opposed the bill on the same grounds as in 1958, arguing that the trust funds could not support such liberalization of entitlements. Representative Forand (D-RI) supported the bill, but complained that it did not include any provisions for health care for the aged or disabled. Representative Franklin Roosevelt, Jr. (D-NY), endorsed the bill, but emphasized that this legislation would not lead to health care for the aged. He stated his opposition to socialized medicine, but wanted to know when something would be done to address the issue of national health care. The legislators then took turns offering their support to the national health care movement and the plan advocated by Representative Forand. By this point, H.R. 12580 had become a side issue. The bill passed the House on June 22, 1960 by a vote of 381-23.[26]

The Senate Finance Committee took up H.R. 12580 on June 28, 1960. Hearings were held through June 30. HEW Secretary Arthur Flemming testified on June 29 and the AMA contingent followed on June 30. Flemming stated that the administration supported the entire bill. However, Flemming's sincerity was called into question by Senator George Smathers (D-FL) who believed that the administration, and Flemming in particular, had been dragging their heels, hoping the bill would die in committee in either the House or the Senate. Dr. Leonard Larson and Dr. C.J. Stetler testified on the behalf of the AMA and they emphasized their opposition to the bill in passing, instead taking this opportunity to reiterate their opposition to socialized medicine. Nelson Cruikshank of the AFL testified in support of the DI provisions of the bill, praising the TWP provision as an effective complement to vocational rehabilitation.[27]

The committee met in executive session from August 10 through August 19, 1960 when it reported the bill to the Senate. The Senate debated the bill from August 20 through August 23 and focused on the proposed increases in federal bloc grants to state welfare programs. There was little dissension over the DI provisions. The bill passed the Senate August 23 by a vote of 91-2. The lone dissenters were Senators Barry Goldwater (R-AZ) and Strom Thurmond (D-SC). Neither Goldwater nor Thurmond joined the debate over the bill, but Thurmond entered his objections into the *Congressional Record* after the vote. He believed that the DI provisions in the bill diminished or inhibited the growth of the private disability insurance industry as well as private pension funds. He also asserted that beneficiaries were being offered too great an incentive to stay on the federal dole.[28]

The Conference Committee on H.R. 12580 met on August 25, 1960, and agreed with little debate on a final version of the bill, which was quickly adopted by both the House and the Senate by lopsided majorities. When signed into law by the President, H.R. 12580—now PL 86-778—lowered the minimum age requirement for disability benefits to 18, initiated the Trial Work Period provisions and eliminated the 5-month waiting period to qualify for disability benefits if the onset date was within five years of a prior entitlement's termination. Eisenhower made no public statement concerning this legislation. The ongoing presidential campaign between John F Kennedy and Richard Nixon dominated the news and PL 86-778 went largely unnoticed. Eisenhower deliberately called more attention to the recently enacted Kerr-Mills program of federal grants to the states for medical care to the elderly. Kerr-Mills provided assistance for those not on welfare, but unable to afford proper medical services. It was not exactly what Eisenhower had had in mind in his previous efforts to address the issue of health care for seniors, but he believed it was a step in the right direction. The Social Security Amendments of 1960 were simply background noise to the ongoing health care debate and presidential campaigns.[29]

Personally, Eisenhower disdained the DI provisions of the new law. He felt that the vocational rehabilitation principle had been undermined in every possible way. Allowing workers as young as the age of

18 to receive cash payments would only encourage sloth. While the TWP would allow those with initiative to get jobs and to work, it did not mean that they were necessarily learning a new vocation. Getting a new job and getting a new career were completely different things. Pubic reaction to PL 86-778 was favorable; it was touted as bigger pensions for more people that were easier to obtain. It played well for the legislators in an election year, but it only affected a minute segment of the population, and, as such, it was not considered national, or even breaking, news.[30]

References: Chapter Four

1) Social Security Administration, *POMS-Program Operations Manual System* (Baltimore: SSA CD-ROM Publications, May 2000), RS 01404.300; Bernstein 12; Ambrose 158; *Pub Potus, 1954*, 62-68; Adams 8-9. (*POMS-Program Operations Manual System* hereinafter referred to as POMS)

2) Johnson and Porter, 545.

3) Johnson and Porter, 550.

4) Johnson and Porter, 532, 534.

5) *Pub Potus, 1956*, 618.

6) Branyan and Larsen, 814; *Pub Potus 1957*, 38-59.

7) 103 *CD* (1957), D152, D166; 103 *CR* (1957), 4700-4701; U.S., Congress, House of Representatives, Committee on Ways and Means, *Social Security Act—Disability Determination*, House Report 277, 85th Congress, 1st Session, 1957, 1374-1376.

8) 103 *CD* (1957), D352, D358, D415, D171; 103 *CR* (1957), 10884; House Report 277; U.S., Congress, Senate, Committee on Finance, *Social Security Act—Disability Determination*, Senate Report 455, 85th Congress, 1st Session, 1957, 1-3.

9) *Pub Potus, 1958*, 51-2.

10) 104 CD (1958), D363; U.S., Congress, House of Representatives, Committee on Ways and Means, *Social Security Amendments of 1958*, House Report 2288, 85th Congress, 2nd Session, 1958, 13.

11) 104 *CD* (1958), D363; U.S., Congress, House of Representatives, Committee on Ways and Means, *Social Security Legislation:*

Hearings on H.R. 13549 and All Titles of the Social Security Act, 85th Congress, 2nd Session, 1958, 3-39.

12) *Hearings on H.R. 13549,* 368-375.

13) 104 *CD* (1958), D457, 462, 467, 477, 483, 492, 496, 497, 501, 503; 104 CR (1958), 15730-1; House Report 2288, 13.

14) 104 *CD* (1958), D514; 104 *CR* (1958), 15732-15736, 15740, 15742-3, 15751.

15) 104 *CD* (1958), 514; 104 *CR* (1958), 15775-7.

16) 104 *CD* (1958), D550; U.S., Congress, Senate, Committee on Finance, *Social Security Act Amendments of 1958: Hearings on H.R. 13549,* 85th Congress, 2nd Session, 1958, 111-145.

17) 104 *CD* (1958), D556, 560, 566.

18) 104 *CD* (1958), D571, 573, 578, 583; *CR* 17957, 17798-9, 17970.

19) 104 *CD* (1958), D583, 592; *CR* 19074-5, 19715.

20) *Pub Potus, 1958,* 661.

21) *POMS,* RS 01404.300; *New York Times,* August 30, 1958, 1, 4, 16; *Time Magazine,* September 1, 1958, 16; *Pub Potus* 1958, 661.

22) *U.S. News and World Report,* August 8, 1958, 42-44; *U.S. News and World Report,* August 29, 1958, 34-35; *U.S. News and World Report,* December 19, 1958, 95; *Time Magazine,* November 3, 1958, 4.

23) *Pub Potus, 1959,* 102-3.

24) *Pub Potus, 1960,* 195.

25) 106 *CD* (1960), D123-D321, D361, 363; 106 *CR* (1960), 12310, 13808-9.

26) 106 *CD* (1960) 383-390; 106 *CR* (1960), 13808-9, 13814, 13818-13829.

27) 106 *CD* (1960), D408, 414, 420; U.S., Congress, Senate, Committee on Finance, *Social Security Act Amendments of 1960: Hearings on H.R. 12580*, 86th Congress, 2nd Session, 1960, 42-80, 83-424.

28) 106 *CD* (1960), D451, 452, 455; 106 *CR* (1960), 16740, 16856-17225, 17235.

29) 106 *CD* (1960), D471, 476, 464, 467, 468; 106 *CR* (1960), 17874; Social Security Administration, *Chronology of Social Security Events*. Washington, D.C.; mwww.ba.ssa.

gov/history/chrono.html; *New York Times*, August 29, 1960, 1, 18.

30) *U.S. News and World Report*, January 11, 1960, 100-103; and September 5, 1960, 42-3.

Conclusions

President Eisenhower left office in January 1961. During his second term, the Social Security program had been liberalized in ways that he never imagined possible in 1953, or even 1956. He watched in retirement as a national health insurance plan was finally enacted in 1965. He watched Democratic President Lyndon Johnson sign the Medicare/Medicaid bill into law as a grinning Harry Truman stood behind him. Eisenhower's efforts to pass similar bills were forgotten and the Democrats took credit for offering even more aid to the sick and elderly. In his memoirs, Eisenhower deliberately distanced himself from the Social Security reforms that had taken place during his administration. Even the scholarship on his presidency rarely mentions Social Security, with the exception of his expansion of the OASI program. This was by design. Eisenhower did not go down in history as a great social insurance reformer because he did not want his name forever linked to the DI program, a program he did not like, and the creation of the modern welfare state. To this end, he was successful.[1]

As early as 1952, Eisenhower warned Republicans that the party needed to adopt a more moderate, more progressive, social agenda to match the current mood of the nation. In an attempt to do just that, he laid a foundation with the 1954 amendments to the Social Security Act. Eisenhower and the Republicans failed to capitalize on this initiative, however, and the Democrats got credit for everything that came after. The popularity of these reforms were reflected at the polls and it was not an accident that all of the Social Security reforms in the 1950's were passed during election years. Eisenhower himself remained personally popular and was re-elected to a second term, but

Republicans rapidly lost seats in the House and Senate until they were outnumbered almost 2 to 1 in the 86th Congress. The infighting between the moderate and conservative factions robbed the Republican Party of an opportunity to dominate in the 1950's after 20 years of Democratic control.[2]

The program that exists today is far from the one that Eisenhower or any of his contemporaries envisioned. But Social Security, like everything else, has evolved over time to meet the current demands of society. A major shortcoming of the 1956 amendments was that they did not realistically address the needs of the white-collar professional or the mentally ill. They also did not address the health insurance needs of the disabled; it was not humanly possible in 1956, as it is now, to live on a Social Security Disability payment and to afford health care.

The program created by the 1954 amendments was based on an overly optimistic assumption about human nature. It was taken for granted that blue-collar workers would embrace the opportunity for vocational rehabilitation, when in fact the opposite has been true. While it wouldn't be fair to say that blue-collar workers in general lacked the aptitude to learn new skills, the fact remains that there has been a reluctance to retrain. One's vocation defines one's very nature. To learn a new vocation struck at the very core of one's self image and such a drastic change was often untenable. The inherent dislike at being told what to do by the federal government combined with the inadequate resources of the vocational rehabilitation agencies to exacerbate the problem. Henry Viscardi and the employees of Abilities, Inc, were the exceptions. The Trial Work Period provision of the 1960 amendments was a much more palatable alternative because it returned to the worker the responsibility for returning to viable employment. While more palatable, it was not necessarily in the best interests of the worker. I agree with Eisenhower that getting a job is not the same as getting a career. Most disabled workers wanting to return to work need guidance, but whether the government should assume this responsibility is the crux of the debate.[3]

The DI program, as enacted in 1956, contradicted itself. The law often conflicted with the ideology it was supposed to promote. Entitlement was restricted to people aged fifty or older, which undermined the vocational rehabilitation principle. The rehabilitation approach never took hold because the program was designed to cater to younger applicants, but only older applicants could qualify. The overall success of social insurance in America depended upon an orderly partnership between private employers and the federal government. Employers handled the costs of health care, employers and the federal government financed the costs of retirement. This system reduced social policy to three main objectives: the encouragement of employment through macroeconomics, the maintenance and expansion of Social Security through competent administration and the rehabilitation of those outside the labor force through professionally applied social services. The system as created in 1956 has succeeded in two of the three objectives, failing only in the area of vocational rehabilitation.[4]

The DI program and the expansion of covered professions under the OASI program, for all its attractiveness and ugliness to Eisenhower, served, and continues to serve, a very important purpose. The overall size of the federal bureaucracy has grown, but in the case of Social Security it has become more efficient. This is a direct result of the program being enforced from the top down while other state and local programs, such as unemployment and welfare, are operated in the reverse. The funds to operate the Social Security Administration are derived from the Trust Funds and the overhead is only .6 percent of all the FICA tax collected.[5] The minimal overhead is a direct benefit of the federal government's ability to incorporate an existing apparatus for decision-making at the state level into a federal program.[6]

The OASDI programs have significantly reduced the number of Americans living under the poverty level as they now provide 40 percent of the total income for the aged and disabled. In 1959, 35 percent of Americans lived below the poverty level. By 1995, this figure had dropped to 10.5 percent. Social Security keeps 13.5 million people out of poverty annually.[7] There are situations where the DI program has literally saved people's lives. People often cannot afford private disability insurance or do not work at jobs that extend disability coverage. Social Security can, and has, spared many from living on the subsistence level benefits offered by welfare and relieved the states of the burden of caring for these individuals. The federal government turned out to be the perfect instrument to administer a disability program, especially in light of today's global economy. The uniformity in claim determinations, benefit calculations and administrative procedures has solved the problem of mobile workers and the need to provide equitable service to every community in the entire country.[8]

Social Security was never meant to be the cure all for society's ills. It was only meant to alleviate some of the sting of calamity, not eliminate it all together. The core of the program is still that same American ideal that each person has to take care of him or herself. A person still has to find a job, have a career, earn a sufficient wage to provide for a satisfactory benefit amount and plan for the private supplements needed to survive in the event of disaster. The most obvious shortcoming of the program is the problem of varying regional costs of living. Living in the New York metropolitan area is vastly more expensive than living in rural Nebraska, but DI benefit calculations do not take this into consideration. The knee-jerk solution is for a beneficiary to simply move to a locality where he can afford to live, but for any number of reasons, it is not always that easy.[9]

The story of Social Security in the 1950's is wrought with irony. Walter George, a senator Franklin Roosevelt tried to purge as an anti New Dealer, put the finishing touches on the greatest of the New Deal programs, something Roosevelt could not accomplish on his own. Resisting George's efforts at expanding the most popular American benefits program was a President who wanted to go down in history as a progressive. This suggests that the adoption of the DI program was an accident of politics rather than the natural progression of society. The 1954 amendments to the Social Security Act marked the beginning of the slippery slope into the modern welfare state. It is fair to say that Eisenhower let the genie out of the bottle, but only because he assumed he could control it. Eisenhower robbed himself of a great legacy by distancing himself from Social Security reform and selectively omitting his role in it from his memoirs. From my perspective, we are much better off with the Social Security Disability program than we would have been without it.

References: Conclusion

1) Lyndon Baines Johnson. *The Vantage Point: Perspectives on the Presidency, 1963-1969* (New York: Holt, Rinehart and Winston, 1971), 219; Eric F. Goldman. *The Tragedy of Lyndon Johnson* (New York: Alfred A. Knopf, Inc, 1969), 295-296; Eisenhower in his own memoirs, and in the works of his most prominent scholars, such as Reichard, Ambrose and Richardson, give Social Security reform scant attention, if any at all.

2) Bernstein, 12.

3) This point is based on my personal observations made as a claims representative with the Social Security Administration since 1991. The application process and format of questioning has changed little since the Eisenhower administration.

4) Berkowitz, 166, 192.

5) Social Security Administration, *What Are Social Security's Administrative Costs?* Washington, D.C.;

   mwww.ba.ssa.gov/policy/pubs/bgpAdmCost.htm, 1999.

6) Marmor, Mashaw and Harvey, 46; *What Are Social Security's Administrative Costs?*

7) Social Security Administration, *How Does Social Security Help Americans?* Washington, D.C.;

   mwww.ba.ssa.gov/policy/pubs/bgpRevOASDI.htm, 1999.

8) *How Does Social Security Help Americans?*

9) Marmor, Mashaw and Harvey, 22.

Bibliography

Adams, Sherman. *First Hand Report: The Story of the Eisenhower Administration*. New York: Harper and Brothers, 1961.

Alexander, Charles. *Holding the Line: The Eisenhower Era, 1952-1961*. Bloomington: Indiana University Press, 1975.

Ambrose, Stephen. *Eisenhower: The President*. New York: Simon and Schuster, 1984.

Berkowitz, Edward. *America's Welfare State, From Roosevelt to Reagan*. Baltimore: Johns Hopkins University Press, 1991.

Bernstein, Merton, and Joan Brodshaug-Bernstein. *Social Security: The System That Works*. New York: Basic Books, 1988.

Boller, Paul, Jr. *Congressional Anecdotes*. New York: Oxford University Press, 1991.

Boller, Paul, Jr. *Presidential Anecdotes*. New York: Viking Penguin, 1982.

Boller, Paul, Jr. *Presidential Campaigns*. New York: Oxford University Press, 1985.

Branyan, Robert, and Lawrence Larsen, eds. *The Eisenhower Administration, 1953-1961: A Documentary History*. 2 Vols. New York: Random House, 1971.

Committee on Economic Security. *Report to the President*. Washington, D.C.: U.S. Government Printing Office, 1935.

Cotton, Norris. *In the Senate: Amidst the Conflict and the Turmoil*. New York: Dodd, Mead and Company, 1978.

David, Sheri. "Eisenhower and the American Medical Association: A Coalition Against the Elderly." *Dwight D Eisenhower: Soldier, President, Statesman*. Ed. Joann Krieg. New York: Greenwood Press, 1987. 57-65.

DeGregorio, William. *The Complete Book of U.S. Presidents*. New York: Barricade Books, 1991.

Donovan, Robert. *Eisenhower: The Inside Story*. New York: Harper and Brothers, 1956.

Douglas, Paul. *In the Fullness of Time: The Memoirs of Paul H Douglas*. New York: Harcourt Brace Jovanich, 1972.

Eisenhower to Earl Schaefer, 3 Feb 1954, at www.ba.ssa.gov/history/ikeletter.html.

Eisenhower, Dwight. *The White House Years, Vol I, Mandate for Change, 1953-1956*. Garden City, NY: Doubleday and Company, 1963.

Eisenhower, Dwight. *The White House Years, Vol 2, Waging Peace, 1956-1961*. Garden City, NY: Doubleday and Company, 1965.

Ferrell, Robert, ed. *The Diary of James C Hagerty: Eisenhower in Mid-Course, 1954-1955*. Bloomington: Indiana University Press, 1983.

Fite, Gilbert. *Richard B Russell, Jr.: Senator From Georgia*. Chapel Hill: University of North Carolina Press, 1991.

Gilbert, Robert. *The Mortal Presidency: Illness and Anguish in the White House*. New York: Basic Books, 1992.

Goldman, Eric. *The Crucial Decade—and After: America, 1945-1960*. New York: Random House, 1960.

Goldman, Eric. *The Tragedy of Lyndon Johnson*. New York: Alfred A. Knopf, 1969.

Greenstein, Fred. *The Hidden-Hand Presidency: Eisenhower as Leader*. New York: Basic Books, 1982.

Hardeman, D.B. and Bacon, Donald. *Rayburn: A Biography*. Houston: Gulf Publishing, 1987.

Johnson, Donald and Kirk Porter, eds. *National Party Platforms: 1840-1960*. Urbana: University of Illinois Press, 1961.

Johnson, Lyndon Baines. *The Vantage Point: Perspectives on the Presidency, 1963-1969*. New York: Holt, Rinehart and Winston, 1971.

Leuchtenburg, William E. *Franklin D Roosevelt and the New Deal, 1932-1940*. New York: Harper and Row, 1963.

Marmor, Theodore, Jerry Mashaw and Philip Harvey. *America's Misunderstood Welfare State: Persistent Myths, Eduring Realities*. New York: Basic Books, 1990.

Martin, Joseph. *My First Fifty Years in Politics*. New York: McGraw Hill, 1960.

New York Times, 1953-1961.

Parmet, Herbert. *Eisenhower and the American Crusades*. New York: MacMillan Company, 1972.

Public Papers of the President: Eisenhower, 1953-1961. Washington, D.C.: U.S. Government Printing Office, 1958-1961.

Reichard, Gary. *The Reaffirmation of Republicanism: Eisenhower and the 83rd Congress*. Knoxville: University of Tennessee Press, 1975.

Richardson, Elmo. *The Presidency of Dwight D Eisenhower*. Lawrence: Regents Press of Kansas, 1979.

Schlesinger, Arthur, Jr. *The Age of Roosevelt*. Vol. 2, *The Coming of the New Deal*. Cambridge: Houghton Mifflin Company, 1958.

Social Security Administration. *A Brief History of Social Security*. Washington, D.C.: U.S. Government Printing Office, SSA Publication No. 21-059, 1995.

Social Security Administration. *Chronology of Social Security Events*. Washington, D.C.: mwww.ba.ssa.gov/history/chrono.html, 1999.

Social Security Administration. *Fast Facts and Figures About Social Security*. Washington, D.C.: U.S. Government Printing Office, SSA Publication No. 13-11785, 1999.

Social Security Administration. *How Does Social Security Help Americans?* Washington, D.C.: mwww.ba.ssa.gov/policy/pubs/bgpRevOASDI.htm, 1999.

Social Security Administration. *POMS-Program Operations Manual System*. Baltimore: SSA CD-ROM Publications, May 2000.

Social Security Administration. *What Are Social Security's Administrative Costs?* Washington, D.C.: mwww.ba.ssa.gov/policy/pubs/bgpAdmCost.htm, 1999.

Tananbaum, Duane. *The Bricker Amendment Controversy: A Test of Eisenhower's Political Leadership*. Ithaca, NY: Cornell University Press, 1988.

TIME Magazine, 1953-1961.

U.S, Congress. *Compilation of the Social Security Laws, Including the Social Security Act, as Amended, and Related Enactments*. Public Law 74-271. Washington D.C.: U.S. Government Printing Office, 1999.

U.S., Congress. *Congressional Record*, 83rd to 86th Congress, 1953-1960.

U.S., Congress. *Congressional Record—Daily Digest*, 83rd to 86th Congress, 1953-1960.

U.S., Congress. House of Representatives. Committee on Ways and Means. *Social Security*. House Document 225, 83rd Congress, 1st Session, 1953.

U.S., Congress. House of Representatives. Committee on Ways and Means. *Social Security Act Amendments of 1954: Hearings on H.R. 7199*. 83rd Congress, 2nd Session, 1954.

U.S., Congress. House of Representatives. Committee on Ways and Means. *Social Security Act Amendments of 1954*. House Report 1698, 83rd Congress, 2nd Session, 1954.

U.S., Congress. House of Representatives. Committee on Ways and Means. *Social Security Act Amendments of 1955*. House Report 1189, 84th Congress, 1st Session, 1955.

U.S., Congress. House of Representatives. Committee on Ways and Means. *Social Security Act   Amendments of 1956*. Conference Report 2936, 84th Congress, 2nd Session, 1956.

U.S., Congress. House of Representatives. Committee on Ways and Means. *Social Security Act Amendments of 1958*. House Report 2288, 85th Congress, 2nd Session, 1958.

U.S., Congress. House of Representatives. Committee on Ways and Means. *Social Security Act—Disability Determination*. House Report 277, 85th Congress, 1st Session, 1957.

U.S., Congress. House of Representatives. Committee on Ways and Means. *Social Security Legislation: Hearings on H.R. 13549 and All Titles of the Social Security Act*. 85th Congress, 2nd Session, 1958.

U.S., Congress. Senate. Committee on Finance. *Social Security Act Amendments of 1954: Hearings on H.R. 9366*. 83rd Congress, 2nd Session, 1954.

U.S., Congress. Senate. Committee on Finance. *Social Security Act Amendments of 1955: Hearings on H.R. 7225*. 84th Congress, 2nd Session, 1956.

U.S., Congress. Senate. Committee on Finance. *Social Security Act Amendments of 1958: Hearings on H.R. 13549.* 85th Congress, 2nd Session, 1958.

U.S., Congress. Senate. Committee on Finance. *Social Security Act Amendments of 1960: Hearings on H.R. 12580.* 86th Congress, 2nd Session, 1960.

U.S. Congress. Senate. Committee on Finance. *Social Security Act— Disability Determination.* Senate Report 455, 85th Congress, 1st Session, 1957.

U.S., Congress. Senate. Committee on Finance. *Social Security Amendments of 1956.* Senate Report 2133, 84th Congress, 2nd Session, 1956.

U.S. News and World Report, 1953-1961.